**Concise Guides
for the Next Century**

Spelling
Made Simple

**Concise Guides
for the Next Century**

Spelling
Made Simple

**Compiled by
Hayden Mead, Ph.D.**

Developed by The Philip Lief Group, Inc.

BERKLEY BOOKS, NEW YORK

SPELLING MADE SIMPLE

A Berkley Book / published by arrangement with
The Philip Lief Group, Inc.

PRINTING HISTORY
Berkley edition / October 1996

The Putnam Berkley World Wide Web site address is
http://www.berkley.com/berkley

ISBN: 0-425-15524-2

BERKLEY®
Berkley Books are published by The Berkley Publishing Group,
200 Madison Avenue, New York, New York 10016.
BERKLEY and the "B" design
are trademarks belonging to Berkley Publishing Corporation.

PRINTED IN THE UNITED STATES OF AMERICA

10 9 8 7 6 5 4 3 2 1

INTRODUCTION

The *Concise Guides* series consists of six reference workbooks for people who need to communicate effectively both in person and on paper, and who need to find reliable answers quickly and efficiently. The basic rules and helpful learning suggestions presented in *Spelling Made Simple* will provide misspellers and writers of all levels with clear, comprehensive information in a revolutionary new way. As many chronic misspellers have found, it is almost impossible to conduct a quick word search without knowing how to spell a word. Whether for home, business, or educational use, *Spelling Made Simple* is the handiest spelling tool available. It lists entries for both correct spellings (in bold) and incorrect spellings (in regular type), and therefore does not require that you already know the proper spelling of a word before you try to look it up.

Spelling skills are not a reflection of a person's character or competence. Nor do spelling skills indicate a person's ability to think clearly or to write powerfully. However, though it may not seem fair, spelling is a measure of literacy and intellect, and therefore it is an essential skill for both business people and students to master. Poor spelling detracts from potentially good writing by distracting the reader, obscuring otherwise clear ideas and masking the intelligence of the writer. You can overcome the seemingly insurmountable obstacle of poor spelling by referring to the lists of commonly misspelled words presented in *Spelling Made Simple*, and by following the advice below.

Use a dictionary

While *Spelling Made Simple* is the complete source for improved spelling, never forget that your good old dictionary is, and should always be, your prime reference for definitions, pronunciations, and root words. While a dictionary is evidently *not* the ideal place to look up a misspelling, it can help you if your misspelling alphabetically falls anywhere near the proper spelling of the word.

Mnemonic devices

A mnemonic device is a special trick used as a memory aid. By associating a certain phrase or idea with the spelling of a particular word, you can use mnemonics to help you remember that spelling. For example, you might say to yourself that a *secret*ary is someone who can keep a *secret* — which will prevent you from spelling it *secritery* or *secratery*. You can remember that a princi*ple* is a rule, if you say that a princi*pal* is a person because he or she is your *pal*. You might also remember that *desert* has one *s* because there is only one well in the desert, and *dessert* has two because you always want two pieces of pie. Don't forget, however, that mnemonic devices often work best when the trick has a personal meaning for you, so don't be afraid to come up with your own. Though you shouldn't spend time making elaborate associations that may be as hard to remember as the spellings themselves, creating and using your own memory devices can be a quick and fun way to help you with problematic words.

I before E . . .

"*I* before *e*, except after *c*, or when sounding like *ay* as in *neighbor* and *weigh*." Remembering this basic rule will help you correctly spell many commonly misspelled words, such as *friend*, *believe*, *ceiling* and *sleigh*.

As with any general spelling rule, there are, of course, exceptions. For example, *i* comes before *e*, even after *c*, in words like *ancient* or *species*. Words like *seizure*, however, do just the opposite, putting *e* before *i* even though it isn't after *c* and doesn't sound like *ay*. Words like *diet*, in which the *i* and the *e* are pronounced separately, don't follow the rule, either. In addition, the words *either*, *height*, *caffeine*, and *weird*, among others, ignore the rule as well. In stubborn exceptions such as these, you may want to develop your own mnemonic device to remind you of the correct spelling. For example, if you know the spelling of *adrenaline*, you can remember that *caffeine* ends in *-ine* because it has the same effect on your body as adrenal*ine*, and so the last three letters are identical. These exceptions make the "*I* before *e*" rule seem almost hopeless; but for the vast majority of words containing *i* and *e*, it does work. Therefore, we suggest you learn it, if you don't know it already.

Pronouncing words correctly

Spelling Made Simple provides a syllabic breakdown of every word so that you can see the proper pronunciation of trouble words at a glance. Many misspellings result from careless and easily corrected mispronunciations. *Precipitation*, for example, is often spelled as *percipitation* because that is the way many people pronounce it. People who leave out letters or even syllables when they say certain words tend to spell them that way: for example, *choclate* instead of *chocolate*. Knowing the proper pronunciations of words, and being careful to say them, can quickly reduce your number of spelling errors.

Homonyms and homophones

Beware of homonyms and homophones, which can cause mistakes even when you know how to spell them correctly. Homonyms are words with the same spelling but different meanings; homophones are words with similar pronunciations but different spellings and meanings. *Spelling Made Simple* will alert you to potential spelling disasters caused by these words. Homophones and homonyms often escape your word processor's spellchecker, so it is important to be especially careful. Knowing the definitions of words is extremely useful and will help you avoid mix-ups between homonyms and homophones. Using *bridle* when referring to a wedding, for example, would be incorrect, even though *bridle* is an acceptable spelling. The correct word to use here is *bridal*—which sounds like *bridle*, but means "having to do with a wedding" rather than "a part of a horse's harness." Associating the meanings of words with their respective spellings will enable you to differentiate between easily confused terms such as these.

Proofreading

Always proofread. The age-old advice rings true not only to ensure clear, good writing, but to be certain that you have done your best at detecting words that may be spelled incorrectly. You will be surprised at how often you can identify your own mistakes just by rereading and applying your own critical eye to your work. Mistakes due to carelessness or a poor keystroke are inexcusable, especially if you actually know the correct spellings of the words you misspelled. Sometimes a spelling error is missed only because the word is so common your eye doesn't catch it. Reread your material on the computer screen several times; take advantage of your computer's spellchecker; carefully proofread the hardcopy printout; and have a friend read it over just to troubleshoot for errant spellings. If ever in doubt about a spelling, consult *Spelling Made Simple*.

**Concise Guides
for the Next Century**

Spelling
Made Simple

Aa

aard•vark
abaitment : **a•bate•ment**
abanden : **a•ban•don**
abandin : **a•ban•don**
a•ban•don
abatemant : **a•bate•ment**
a•bate•ment
abayance : **a•bey•ance**
ab•bey
ab•bot
abbott : **ab•bot**
ab•bre•vi•ate
abby : **ab•bey**
abdecate : **ab•di•cate**
ab•dic•ate
ab•do•men
abdomin : **ab•do•men**
aberation : **ab•er•ra•tion**
aberent : **ab•er•rant**
ab•er•rant
ab•er•ra•tion
aberrent : **ab•er•rant**
a•bey•ance
abeyence : **a•bey•ance**
ab•hor
abhorance : **ab•hor•rence**

abhore : **ab•hor**
ab•hor•rence
abismal : **a•bys•mal**
abiss : **a•byss**
ab•ne•gate
abnigate: **ab•ne•gate**
abnoxious : **ob•nox•ious**
abolission : **ab•o•li•tion**
ab•o•li•tion
abomanable :
   a•bom•i•na•ble
abominabel :
   a•bom•i•na•ble
a•bom•i•na•ble
abor : **ab•hor**
aborence : **ab•hor•rence**
aboretion : **abor•tion**
ab•or•ig•i•ne
aboriginee : **ab•or•ig•i•ne**
aboriginey : **ab•or•ig•i•ne**
a•bor•tion
abot : **ab•bot**
abott : **ab•bot**
a•brade
abraid : **a•brade**
abregate : **ab•ro•gate**

abreviate : **ab•bre•vi•ate**
a•bridg•ment
abrigement :
  a•bridg•ment
a•broad
abrode : **a•broad**
ab•ro•gate
absalutely : **ab•so•lute•ly**
ab•sence
absense : **ab•sence**
ab•so•lute•ly
absorbant : **ab•sor•bent**
ab•sor•bent
absorbtion : **ab•sorp•tion**
ab•sorp•tion
abstinance : **ab•sti•nence**
ab•sti•nence
ab•surd
a•bun•dance
a•bun•dant
abundence : **a•bun•dance**
abundent : **a•bun•dant**
a•but•ment
abuttment : **a•but•ment**
a•bys•mal
a•byss
ac•a•dem•i•cal•ly
academicly :
  ac•a•dem•i•cal•ly
ac•cede
acceed : **ac•cede**
accelarate : **ac•cel•er•ate**
ac•cel•er•ate

accelerater :
  ac•cel•er•a•tor
ac•cel•er•a•tor
ac•cent
ac•cept (receive); **ex•cept**
  (not including)
ac•cep•tance
acceptence : **ac•cep•tance**
accesible : **ac•ces•si•ble**
accessable : **ac•ces•si•ble**
accessery : **ac•ces•so•ry**
ac•ces•si•ble
ac•ces•so•ry
ac•cli•mate
ac•com•mo•date
ac•co•lade
accomodate :
  ac•com•mo•date
ac•com•pa•ni•ment
accompanyment :
  ac•com•pa•ni•ment
ac•com•plice
accomplis : **ac•com•plice**
accomplishmant :
  ac•com•plish•ment
ac•com•plish•ment
accordian : **ac•cor•di•on**
accordien : **ac•cor•di•on**
ac•cor•di•on
ac•cord•ing•ly
ac•count•able
accountible :
  ac•count•able
ac•cu•mu•late

ac•cu•rate
ac•cu•sa•to•ry
acent : ac•cent
acessible : ac•cess•i•ble
acheivement :
  a•chieve•ment
achievemant :
  a•chieve•ment
a•chieve•ment
ackolade : ac•co•lade
aclimate : ac•cli•mate
acolade : ac•co•lade
acommodate :
  ac•com•mo•date
acompaniment :
  ac•com•pa•ni•ment
acomplishment :
  ac•com•plish•ment
acording : ac•cord•ing•ly
a•cous•tic
activiteis : ac•tiv•i•ties
ac•tiv•i•ties
actualisation :
  ac•tu•al•iza•tion
ac•tu•al•iza•tion
ac•tu•al•ly
actualy : ac•tu•al•ly
acumulate :
  ac•cu•mu•late
acurate : ac•cu•rate
acusatory : ac•cu•sa•to•ry
acustic : a•cous•tic
ad•den•dum
ad•dict

ad•dic•tion
ad•di•tion
addresee : ad•dress•ee
ad•dress•ee
adendum : ad•den•dum
adict : ad•dict
adiction : ad•dic•tion
adition : ad•di•tion
adjudecate : ad•ju•di•cate
ad•ju•di•cate
adolescance :
  ad•o•les•cence
ad•o•les•cence
adrenalin : a•dren•a•line
a•dren•a•line
adrenoline : a•dren•a•line
adressee : ad•dress•ee
ad•van•ta•geous
advantagous :
  ad•van•ta•geous
advertisemant :
  ad•ver•tise•ment
ad•ver•tise•ment
ad•vice
advise : ad•vice
aer•o•bic
aes•thet•ic; es•thet•ic
af•fect (influence); ef•fect
  (result; bring about)
affeminate : ef•fem•i•nate
afficiency : ef•fi•cien•cy
af•fi•da•vit
afidavit : af•fi•da•vit
aggresive : ag•gres•sive

ag•gres•sive
agressive : **ag•gres•sive**
airobic : **aer•o•bic**
akward : **awk•ward**
al•be•it
albiet : **al•be•it**
albite : **al•be•it**
allotmant : **al•lot•ment**
al•lot•ment
alotment : **al•lot•ment**
al•tar (chapel); **al•ter**
  (change)
al•ter (change); **al•tar**
  (chapel)
am•a•teur
amature : **am•a•teur**
analisis : **anal•y•sis**
analize : **an•a•lyze**
anal•y•sis
an•a•lyze
announcemant :
  an•nounce•ment
an•nounce•ment
anouncement :
  an•nounce•ment
antecedant : **an•te•ced•ent**
an•te•ced•ent

aparently : **ap•par•ent•ly**
apearance : **ap•pear•ance**
apointment :
  ap•point•ment
apon : **u•pon**
apossum : **o•pos•sum**
ap•par•ent•ly
ap•pear•ance
appearence :
  ap•pear•ance
ap•point•ment
ap•pro•pri•ate
appropriet :
  ap•pro•pri•ate
apropriate :
  ap•pro•pri•ate
ardvark : **aard•vark**
arguement : **ar•gu•ment**
ar•gu•ment
asthetic : **aes•thet•ic**
autum : **au•tumn**
au•tumn
auxilary : **aux•il•ia•ry**
aux•il•ia•ry
auxiliery : **aux•il•ia•ry**
awk•ward
axcent : **ac•cent**

Bb

babbel : **bab•ble**
bab•ble
babboon : **ba•boon**
bacalaureate :
　bac•ca•lau•re•ate
baccalaurate :
　bac•ca•lau•re•ate
bac•ca•lau•re•ate
baccelarate :
　bac•ca•lau•re•ate
bac•cha•nal
baccnal : **bac•cha•nal**
bachelar : **bach•e•lor**
bach•e•lor
bachelorate :
　bac•ca•lau•re•ate
back•ped•al
backpetal : **back•ped•al**
backpetle : **back•ped•al**
backslaping :
　back•slap•ping
back•slap•ping
bad•min•ton
badmitten : **bad•min•ton**
badmitton : **bad•min•ton**
baffelmant : **baf•fle•ment**

baf•fle•ment
baflement : **baf•fle•ment**
ba•gel
bagle : **ba•gel**
bail (prison payment);
　bale (bundle)
bail•out
bale (bundle); **bail** (prison
　payment)
baleout : **bail•out**
balerina : **bal•le•ri•na**
balistic : **bal•lis•tic**
ballerena : **bal•le•ri•na**
bal•le•ri•na
bal•lis•tic
ballistick : **bal•lis•tic**
bal•loon
baloon : **bal•loon**
ba•nana
bannana : **ba•nana**
baptise : **bap•tize**
bap•tize
baracks : **bar•racks**
bar•bar•ian
barbarien : **bar•bar•ian**
bar•bar•ous

barbearian : **bar•bar•ian**
barberous : **bar•bar•ous**
bare (unconcealed); **bear**
   (animal; carry)
bare•ly (hardly); **bar•ley**
   (grain)
bareness : **bar•on•ess**
barette : **bar•rette**
bar•gain
bargin : **bar•gain**
barly : **bare•ly** (hardly);
   bar•ley (grain)
barones : **bar•on•ess**
bar•on•ess
bar•racks
barrete : **bar•rette**
bar•rette
bar•tend•er
bartendor : **bar•tend•er**
ba•si•cal•ly
basicaly : **ba•si•cal•ly**
batlement : **bat•tle•ment**
batlefield : **bat•tle•field**
battlefeild : **bat•tle•field**
bat•tle•field
battlemant : **bat•tle•ment**
bat•tle•ment
beagal : **bea•gle**
bea•gle
bear (animal; carry); **bare**
   (unconcealed)
beastial : **bes•tial**
beau•ti•ful
beautifull : **beau•ti•ful**

bed•ding
beding : **bed•ding**
beegle : **bea•gle**
begar : **beg•gar**
beg•gar
begger : **beg•gar**
begile : **be•guile**
be•gin•ning
begining : **be•gin•ning**
be•grudge
begruge : **be•grudge**
be•guile
beleif : **be•lief**
beleivable : **be•liev•able**
beleive : **be•lieve**
be•lief
believabel : **be•liev•able**
be•liev•able
be•lieve
benadiction :
   ben•e•dic•tion
ben•e•dic•tion
ben•e•fi•cial
benidiction :
   ben•e•dic•tion
benificial : **ben•e•fi•cial**
benefisial : **ben•e•fi•cial**
benevolance :
   be•nev•o•lence
be•nev•o•lence
bereavemant :
   be•reave•ment
be•reave•ment

bereavment :
  be•reave•ment
bereevement :
  be•reave•ment
berlesque : **bur•lesque**
berth : **birth**
beseige : **be•siege**
besieg : **be•siege**
be•siege
bes•tial
bestiel : **bes•tial**
bicentenial :
  bi•cen•ten•ni•al
bi•cen•ten•ni•al
bicentenniel :
  bi•cen•ten•ni•al
bicicle : **bi•cy•cle**
bi•cy•cle
bil•ious
bilous : **bil•ious**
binevolence :
  be•nev•o•lence
bio•de•grad•able
biodegradeable :
  bio•de•grad•able
bipass : **by•pass**
birth
bi•sex•u•al
bisiness : **busi•ness**
bi•son
bizare : **bi•zarre**
bi•zarre
bizzare : **bi•zarre**
black•mail

blackmale : **black•mail**
blas•phe•mous
blasphemus :
  blas•phe•mous
blasphimous :
  blas•phe•mous
bleach
bleech : **bleach**
blisful : **bliss•ful**
blisfull : **bliss•ful**
bliss•ful
blissfull : **bliss•ful**
blous : **blouse**
blouse
blowse : **blouse**
bluberry : **blue•ber•ry**
blue•ber•ry
bluebery : **blue•ber•ry**
blured : **blurred**
blurred
board (length of wood):
  bored (uninterested)
boarder : **bor•der**
boardom : **bore•dom**
bodacias : **bo•da•cious**
bo•da•cious
bodygard : **body•guard**
body•guard
bois•ter•ous
boisterus : **bois•ter•ous**
boistirous : **bois•ter•ous**
bolder : **boul•der**
bongalow : **bun•ga•low**
bonteous : **boun•te•ous**

boorbin : **bour•bon**

boose : **booze**

booze

bor•der

bored

boreder : **bor•der**

bore•dom

boredome : **bore•dom**

bor•ough (city section);
   bur•row (dig)

borower : **bor•row•er**

bor•row•er

botal : **bot•tle**

bot•a•ny

botle : **bot•tle**

botny : **bot•a•ny**

bot•tle

boukay : **bou•quet**

boul•der

bound•a•ry

boundry : **bound•a•ry**

boun•te•ous

bountious : **boun•te•ous**

bouqeut : **bou•quet**

bou•quet

bourbin : **bour•bon**

bour•bon

bourgasie : **bour•geoi•sie**

bourgeiousie :
   bour•geoi•sie

bour•geoi•sie

bourgeosie : **bour•geoi•sie**

bourgeozie : **bour•geoi•sie**

boutiqe : **bou•tique**

bou•tique

bowlder : **boul•der**

boyancy : **buoy•an•cy**

bracolli : **broc•co•li**

brake (stop); **break**
   (come apart)

brakeage : **break•age**

breach

bread : **breed**

break•age

breath

breaze : **breeze**

breech : **breach**

breed

breeth : **breath**

breeze

brevaty : **brev•i•ty**

brev•i•ty

brid•al (wedding); **bri•dle**
   (restrain)

bridel : **brid•al** (wedding);
   bri•dle (restrain)

bri•dle (restrain); **brid•al**
   (wedding)

bright

bright•en

briliance : **bril•liance**

bril•liance

brillience : **bril•liance**

brite : **bright**

briten : **bright•en**

broccali : **broc•co•li**

broc•co•li

brocoli : **broc•co•li**

brocolli : **broc•co•li**
brouse : **browse**
browse
bucaneer : **buc•ca•neer**
buc•ca•neer
buckaneer : **buc•ca•ner**
bufalo : **buf•fa•lo**
bufet : **buf•fet**
buf•fa•lo
buffay : **buf•fet**
buf•fet
bugal : **bu•gle**
bu•gle
buletin : **bul•le•tin**
bulletan : **bul•le•tin**
bul•le•tin
bungalo : **bun•ga•low**
bun•ga•low
buoy•an•cy
buoyency : **buoy•an•cy**
buracracy :
    bu•reau•cra•cy
bu•reau•cra•cy
bureaucrasy :
    bu•reau•cra•cy
bur•ied

burito : **bur•ri•to**
burlesk : **bur•lesque**
bur•lesque
burocracy :
    bu•reau•cra•cy
burow : **bor•ough**
    (city section); **bur•row**
    (dig)
bur•ri•to
burritto : **bur•ri•to**
bur•row (dig); **bor•ough**
    (city section)
buryed : **bur•ied**
busines : **busi•ness**
busi•ness
bussiness : **busi•ness**
buteful : **beau•ti•ful**
buterflies : **but•ter•flies**
but•ter•flies
butterflys : **but•ter•flies**
buy•ing
bycicle : **bi•cy•cle**
bying : **buy•ing**
by•pass
bysexual : **bi•sex•u•al**
byson : **bi•son**

Cc

caleidoscope :
ka•lei•do•scope
cal•en•dar
calender : **cal•en•dar**
camomile : **cham•o•mile**
cam•paign
campain : **cam•paign**
campane : **cam•paign**
capichino : **cap•puc•ci•no**
cap•i•tal
capitel : **cap•i•tal**
capitle : **cap•i•tal**
cappacino : **cap•puc•ci•no**
cap•puc•ci•no
capuccino : **cap•puc•ci•no**
caput : **ka•put**
caracteristic :
char•ac•ter•is•tic
car•at; kar•at
caratin : **ker•a•tin**
car•cin•o•gen
cariage : **car•riage**
caril : **car•ol**
carisma : **char•is•ma**
car•ol
carosene : **ker•o•sene**

carot : **car•at; kar•at**
carousle : **car•rou•sel**
car•riage
car•ried
car•rou•sel
carryed : **car•ried**
carsinogen :
car•cin•o•gen
cartelage : **car•ti•lage**
car•ti•lage
cartrage : **car•tridge**
car•tridge
caserole : **cas•se•role**
caset : **cas•sette**
casheer : **cash•ier**
cash•ier
cashualty : **cas•u•al•ty**
cas•se•role
cas•sette
cas•u•al
casuale : **cas•u•al**
casuall : **cas•u•al**
cas•u•al•ty
casuelty : **cas•u•al•ty**
catachism : **cat•e•chism**
cataclism : **cat•a•clysm**
cat•a•clysm

cat•a•comb

catagorise : **cat•e•go•rize**

catagorize : **cat•e•go•rize**

cat•a•log; cat•a•logue

cat•a•logue; cat•a•log

cat•a•lyst

cat•a•ract

ca•tas•tro•phe

catastrophy :
  ca•tas•tro•phe

cat•e•chism

catecomb : **cat•a•comb**

categorise : **cat•e•go•rize**

cat•e•go•rize

cat•e•go•ry

catelog : **cat•a•log;**
  cat•a•logue

cateract : **cat•a•ract**

caterpilar : **cat•er•pil•lar**

cat•er•pil•lar

caterpiller : **cat•er•pil•lar**

catigorize : **cat•e•go•rize**

catigory : **cat•e•go•ry**

catilogue : **cat•a•log;**
  cat•a•logue

catilyst : **cat•a•lyst**

catipiller : **cat•er•pil•lar**

cattel : **cat•tle**

cat•tle

cau•cus

cau•li•flow•er

caus•al

causious : **cau•tious**

cau•tious

cavitee : **cav•i•ty**

cav•i•ty

cawcus : **cau•cus**

cayak : **kay•ak**

cayos : **cha•os**

cease

ce•dar (tree); se•der
  (Passover)

ceese : **cease**

celabrate : **cel•e•brate**

celebrait : **cel•e•brate**

cel•e•brate

ce•les•tial

cel•i•ba•cy

celibasy : **cel•i•ba•cy**

celibrate : **cel•e•brate**

cel•lo

cellofane : **cel•lo•phane**

cel•lo•phane

cel•lu•lar

celluler : **cel•lu•lar**

celophane : **cel•lo•phane**

cemetary : **cem•e•tery**

cem•e•tery

cemical : **chem•i•cal**

cemitary : **cem•e•tery**

cenile : **se•nile**

cen•ser (incense); **cen•sor**
  (examine and remove);
  sen•sor (senses)

cen•sor (examine and
  remove); **cen•ser**
  (incense); **sen•sor**
  (senses)

cen•sus
centagrade : **cen•ti•grade**
cen•ti•grade
cen•ti•me•ter
centrafuge : **cen•tri•fuge**
cen•tri•fuge
ceramony : **cer•e•mo•ny**
cer•e•mo•ny
cerimony : **cer•e•mo•ny**
cerious : **se•ri•ous**
cer•tain
certan : **cer•tain**
chaffeur : **chauf•feur**
chalenge : **chal•lenge**
challinge : **chal•lenge**
cham•o•mile
cham•pagne
champain : **cham•pagne**
champane : **cham•pagne**
champeon : **cham•pi•on**
cham•pi•on
chan•cel•lor
chancelor : **chan•cel•lor**
chandalier : **chan•de•lier**
chan•de•lier
chandilier : **chan•de•lier**
chanel : **chan•nel**
change•a•ble
changible : **change•a•ble**
chan•nel
chanselor : **chan•cel•lor**
cha•os
chap•lain
chaplin : **chap•lain**

char•ac•ter•is•tic
char•coal
charcole : **char•coal**
chareot : **char•i•ot**
char•i•ot
cha•ris•ma
chas•tise
chastize : **chas•tise**
chaufeur : **chauf•feur**
chauf•feur
chau•vin•ist
chavinist : **chau•vin•ist**
cheap
chedar : **ched•dar**
chedder : **ched•dar**
ched•dar
chedder : **ched•dar**
cheeftan : **chief•tain**
cheep : **cheap**
cheif : **chief**
chello : **cel•lo**
chem•i•cal
chew•able
chewible : **chew•able**
chief
chief•tain
chif•fon
chifon : **chif•fon**
childbaring :
   child•bear•ing
child•bear•ing
chiropracter :
   chi•ro•prac•tor
chi•ro•prac•tor

chiv•al•ry
chlor•ine
choclate : **choc•o•late**
choc•o•late
chocolit : **choc•o•late**
choir
cho•les•ter•ol
cholestirol : **cho•les•ter•ol**
choping : **chop•ping**
chop•ping
cho•ral
chorus
chrissen : **chris•ten**
chris•ten
chro•mi•um
chron•ic
chron•i•cle
chro•no•log•i•cal
chry•san•the•mum
cianide : **cy•a•nide**
cibernetics :
   cy•ber•net•ics
ciberpunk : **cy•ber•punk**
cicle : **cy•cle**
ciclone : **cy•clone**
cifer : **ci•pher**
cigaret : **cig•a•rette**
cig•a•rette
cilender : **cyl•in•der**
cimbal : **cym•bal**
cinama : **cin•e•ma**
cin•der
cin•e•ma
cinical : **cyn•i•cal**

ci•pher
cir•cuit
cir•cus
circuss : **cir•cus**
circut : **cir•cuit**
cirhosis : **cir•rho•sis**
ciropractor :
   chi•ro•prac•tor
cir•rho•sis
cis•tern
cisturn : **cis•tern**
cit•a•del
citadell : **cit•a•del**
citazen : **cit•i•zen**
citedel : **cit•a•del**
cit•ies
citys : **cit•ies**
civec : **civ•ic**
civ•ic
civilezation :
   civ•i•li•za•tion
civ•i•li•za•tion
claim
clair•voy•ance
clairvoyence :
   clair•voy•ance
clame : **claim**
clarafication :
   clar•i•fi•ca•tion
clarenet : **clar•i•net**
clarevoyance :
   clair•voy•an•ce
clar•i•fi•ca•tion
clar•i•net

clasify : **clas•si•fy**
clas•si•fy
clastrophobia :
   claus•tro•pho•bia
claustofobia :
   claus•tro•pho•bia
claus•tro•pho•bia
clear•ance
clearanse : **clear•ance**
cleav•age
cleavidge : **cleav•age**
cleche : **cli•ché**
clef
cleff : **clef**
clem•en•cy
clemensy : **clem•en•cy**
cleptomaniac :
   klep•to•man•i•ac
cli•ché
click(noise); **clique**
   (group)
cli•mate
climet : **cli•mate**
cli•nic
clinick : **cli•nic**
clique (group);
   click(noise)
cloisster : **clois•ter**
clois•ter
clorine : **chlo•rine**
clostrophobia :
   claus•tro•pho•bia
cloyster : **clois•ter**
coal

coaks : **coax**
coax
co•caine
cocane : **co•caine**
coercian : **co•er•cion**
co•er•cion
coersion : **co•er•cion**
cognisant : **cog•ni•zant**
cog•ni•zant
coherance : **co•her•ence**
co•her•ence
coin•age
coinege : **coin•age**
cole : **coal**
collaberator :
   col•lab•o•ra•tor
col•lab•o•ra•tor
colleage : **col•league**
col•league
collesterol : **cho•les•ter•ol**
colliflour : **cau•li•flow•er**
collum : **col•umn**
col•umn
combenation :
   com•bi•na•tion
com•bi•na•tion
comedean : **co•me•di•an**
co•me•di•an
com•mis•er•ate
commisirate :
   com•mis•er•ate
commodor :
   com•mo•dore
com•mo•dore

communian :
   com•mu•nion
com•mu•nion
communitee :
   com•mu•ni•ty
com•mu•ni•ty
comodore : **com•mo•dore**
com•pan•ion
companiun : **com•pan•ion**
composhure :
   com•po•sure
com•po•sure
compresion :
   com•pres•sion
com•pres•sion
con•ceiv•able
con•ceive
concievable :
   con•ceiv•able
concieve : **con•ceive**
con•cil•ia•to•ry
concilliatory :
   con•cil•i•a•to•ry
con•cise
concreet : **con•crete**
con•crete
con•de•scend
condesend : **con•de•scend**
con•do•min•i•um
condominnium :
   con•do•min•i•um
confedaracy :
   con•fed•er•a•cy
con•fed•er•a•cy

confederisy :
   con•fed•er•a•cy
con•fer•ence
conferrence :
   con•fer•ence
con•fla•gra•tion
conflagretion :
   con•fla•gra•tion
congragration :
   con•gre•ga•tion
con•gre•ga•tion
conquerer : **con•quer•or**
con•quer•or
con•science
consice : **con•cise**
con•sid•er•able
considerible :
   con•sid•er•able
consise : **con•cise**
constituancey :
   con•stit•u•ency
con•stit•u•ency
con•sul•ate
con•tra•band
con•tra•cep•tive
contraseptive :
   con•tra•cep•tive
contreband :
   con•tra•band
con•triv•ance
contrivence :
   con•triv•ance
contry : **coun•try**
con•vey•ance

conveyence :
   con•vey•ance

corale : **cho•ral**

coroborate :
   cor•rob•o•rate

cor•po•ral

corporel : **cor•po•ral**

corralate : **cor•re•late**

cor•re•late

corrobborate :
   cor•rob•o•rate

cor•rob•o•rate

corus : **chorus**

cosher : **kosh•er**

coun•te•nance

coun•ter•act

counterract : **coun•ter•act**

coun•ter•feit

counterfet : **coun•ter•feit**

countinance :
   coun•te•nance

coun•try

cou•ra•geous

couragious : **cou•ra•geous**

cov•er•age

coverege : **cov•er•age**

cow•ard•ice

cowerdice : **cow•ard•ice**

coxe : **coax**

credibilety :
   cred•i•bil•i•ty

cred•i•bil•i•ty

cre•scen•do

cresendo : **cre•scen•do**

creshendo : **cre•scen•do**

crisanthamum :
   chry•san•the•mum

criticise : **crit•i•cize**

crit•i•cize

cromium : **chro•mi•um**

cronic : **chron•ic**

cronicle : **chron•i•cle**

cronological :
   chro•no•log•i•cal

crus•ta•cean

crustacion : **crus•ta•cean**

crypton : **kryp•ton**

crysanthemum :
   chry•san•the•mum

csar : **czar; tsar**

cui•sine

curcery : **cur•so•ry**

curiosety : **cu•ri•os•i•ty**

cu•ri•os•i•ty

cursery : **cur•so•ry**

cur•so•ry

cy•a•nide

cy•ber•net•ics

cy•ber•punk

cy•cle

cy•clone

cyl•in•der

cym•bal (instrument);
   sym•bol (sign)

cyn•i•cal

czar; tsar

Dd

dabue : **de•but**
dacquiri : **dai•qui•ri**
daf•fo•dil
daffodill : **daf•fo•dil**
dafodil : **daf•fo•dil**
dain•ti•ly
daintly : **dain•ti•ly**
dai•qui•ri
daiquiry : **dai•qui•ri**
daity : **de•i•ty**
dakery : **dai•qui•ri**
damaine : **de•mesne**
dandalion : **dan•de•li•on**
dan•de•li•on
dane : **deign**
danetily : **dain•ti•ly**
dantless : **daunt•less**
daquiri : **dai•qui•ri**
darkan : **dark•en**
dark•en
daunt•less
dayism : **de•ism**
dazle : **daz•zle**
dazzel : **daz•zle**
daz•zle
deaf•en

dealt
dearth
debach : **de•bauch**
de•ba•cle
de•bauch
debue : **de•but**
de•but
decadance : **dec•a•dence**
dec•a•dence
decadense : **dec•a•dence**
decafeinate :
    de•caf•fein•ate
de•caf•fein•ate
decaffenate :
    de•caf•fein•ate
decaffienate :
    de•caf•fein•ate
de•ceive
de•cen•cy
decensy : **de•cen•cy**
decibal : **dec•i•bel**
dec•i•bel
decieve : **de•ceive**
dec•i•mal
decimle : **dec•i•mal**
declair : **de•clare**

de•clare
declasify : **de•clas•si•fy**
declassafy : **de•clas•si•fy**
de•clas•si•fy
decomepress :
   de•com•press
decomission :
   de•com•mis•sion
decommision :
   de•com•mis•sion
de•com•mis•sion
decommition :
   de•com•mis•sion
decompasition :
   de•com•po•si•tion
de•com•po•si•tion
decompres : **de•com•press**
decompresion :
   de•com•pres•sion
de•com•press
de•com•pres•sion
decompretion :
   de•com•pres•sion
dec•o•rous
decorus : **dec•o•rous**
decreace : **de•crease**
de•crease
dedacate : **ded•i•cate**
ded•i•cate
deependent : **de•pen•dent**
defacemant :
   de•face•ment
de•face•ment
defacment : **de•face•ment**

defanite : **def•i•nite**
defen : **deaf•en**
defenceless : **de•fense•less**
de•fen•dant
defendent : **de•fen•dant**
defenition : **def•i•ni•tion**
de•fense•less
de•fer
def•er•ence
deffer : **de•fer**
de•fi•cien•cy
deficiensy : **de•fi•cien•cy**
de•file•ment
defilment : **de•file•ment**
de•fin•able
difinate : **def•i•nite**
defineable : **de•fin•able**
def•i•nite
def•i•ni•tion
defishency : **de•fi•cien•cy**
defrence : **def•er•ence**
deign
dein : **deign**
de•ism
de•i•ty
deleneate : **de•lin•eate**
de•lib•er•ate
delibrate : **de•lib•er•ate**
de•lin•eate
de•lin•quen•cy
dellusion : **de•lu•sion**
delt : **dealt**
de•lu•sion
dem•a•gog; dem•a•gogue

dem•a•gogue; dem•a•gog
demegog : **dem•a•gog;
    dem•a•gogue**
de•mesne
demonatize :
    de•mon•e•tize
de•mon•e•tize
denam : **den•im**
den•im
dependant : **de•pen•dent**
de•pen•dent
depresion : **de•pres•sion**
de•pres•sion
depretion : **de•pres•sion**
deragotory :
    de•rog•a•to•ry
de•rog•a•to•ry
de•scend
desency : **de•cen•cy**
desend : **de•scend**
des•ert (barren land);
    des•sert (food)
de•spair
despare : **de•spair**
des•sert (food); **des•ert**
    (barren land)
detrament : **det•ri•ment**
detrimant : **det•ri•ment**
det•ri•ment
dextarity : **dex•ter•i•ty**
dexteraty : **dex•ter•i•ty**
dex•ter•i•ty
di•a•log; di•a•logue
di•a•logue; di•a•log

diarama : **di•o•ram•a**
diarrea : **di•ar•rhe•a;
    di•ar•rhoe•a**
di•ar•rhoe•a; di•ar•rhe•a
dibacle : **de•ba•cle**
dicease : **dis•ease**
dieing : **dy•ing**
diferent : **dif•fer•ent**
dif•fer•ent
diffrent : **dif•fer•ent**
dif•fu•sion
diffution : **dif•fu•sion**
difusion : **dif•fu•sion**
dillusion : **de•lu•sion**
diminash : **di•min•ish**
di•min•ish
dinamite : **dy•na•mite**
dinasaur : **di•no•saur**
di•no•saur
dinosore : **di•no•saur**
di•o•ra•ma
dire•ful
direfull : **dire•ful**
dirogatory :
    de•rog•a•to•ry
dirth : **dearth**
disapear : **dis•ap•pear**
disapearance :
    dis•ap•pear•ance
disapoint : **dis•ap•point**
dis•ap•pear
dis•ap•pear•ance
dis•ap•point
disastras : **di•sas•trous**

di•sas•trous
disatisfide : **dis•sat•is•fied**
disatisfied : **dis•sat•is•fied**
discend : **de•scend**
disciplin : **dis•ci•pline**
dis•ci•pline
dis•com•bob•u•late
discomebobulate :
   dis•com•bob•u•late
discontineus :
   dis•con•tin•u•ous
dis•con•tin•u•ous
discression : **dis•cre•tion**
dis•cre•tion
discusion : **dis•cus•sion**
dis•cus•sion
dis•ease
disert : **des•ert**
  (barren•land)
disfunction :
   dys•func•tion
disgise : **dis•guise**
dis•guise
disguize : **dis•guise**
dis•il•lu•sion
disilusion : **dis•il•lu•sion**
disipate : **dis•si•pate**
disipline : **dis•ci•pline**
dislectic : **dys•lex•ic**
dislexia : **dys•lex•i•a**
dispair : **de•spair**
disposess : **dis•pos•sess**
dis•pos•sess

disqueitude :
   dis•qui•e•tude
dis•qui•e•tude
dissappearance :
   dis•ap•pear•ance
dissappoint : **dis•ap•point**
dis•sat•is•fied
dissepate : **dis•si•pate**
dis•si•pate
distiler : **dis•till•er**
distillar : **dis•till•er**
dis•till•er
distrophy : **dys•tro•phy**
dockumentation :
   doc•u•men•ta•tion
doctranel : **doc•tri•nal**
doc•tri•nal
doctrinel : **doc•tri•nal**
documentacion :
   doc•u•men•ta•tion
doc•u•men•ta•tion
dontless : **daunt•less**
donut : **dough•nut**
douche
dough•nut
doury : **dow•ry**
doush : **douche**
dow•ry
drib•ble
drible : **drib•ble**
drousy : **drow•sy**
drowsey : **drow•sy**
drow•sy
drumer : **drum•mer**

drum•mer
drunkaness :
   drunk•en•ness
drunkeness :
   drunk•en•ness
drunk•en•ness
du•al (twofold): **du•el**
   (combat)
du•el (combat); **du•al**
   (twofold)
dule : **du•al** (twofold);
   du•el (combat)

dungan : **dun•geon**
dun•geon
dungon : **dun•geon**
dye•ing (to color); **dy•ing**
   (stop living)
dy•ing (stop living);
   dye•ing (to color)
dy•na•mite
dys•func•tion
dys•lex•ia
dys•tro•phy

Ee

eagel : **ea•gle**
ea•gle
earing : **ear•ring**
ear•ring
earthstone : **hearth•stone**
eavesdroper :
   eaves•drop•per
eaves•drop•per
eboney : **eb•o•ny**
ebonie : **eb•o•ny**
eb•o•ny
ebulient : **e•bul•lient**
e•bul•lient
ec•cen•tric
ec•cle•si•as•tic
ecentric : **ec•cen•tric**
é•clair
eclare : **é•clair**
ec•lec•tic
eclectick : **ec•lec•tic**
eclesiastic :
   ec•cle•si•as•tic
ecolagy : **e•col•o•gy**
ecollogy : **e•col•o•gy**
e•col•o•gy
ec•sta•sy

ectacy : **ec•sta•sy**
edibal : **ed•i•ble**
edibel : **ed•i•ble**
ed•i•ble
edipal : **oed•i•pal**
editer : **ed•i•tor**
ed•i•tor
educatian : **ed•u•ca•tion**
ed•u•ca•tion
ee•rie
eery : **ee•rie**
efective : **ef•fec•tive**
efeminate : **ef•fem•i•nate**
efervescent :
   ef•fer•ves•cent
ef•fect (result; bring
   about); **af•fect**
   (influence)
ef•fec•tive
ef•fem•i•nate
effervecent :
   ef•fer•ves•cent
ef•fer•ves•cent
ef•fi•cien•cy
efficiensy : **ef•fi•cien•cy**
ef•fi•cient

effrontary : **ef•fron•tery**
ef•fron•tery
eficiency : **ef•fi•cien•cy**
eficient : **ef•fi•cient**
efrontery : **ef•fron•tery**
e•gal•i•tar•i•an
egaliterian :
    e•gal•i•tar•i•an
eightean : **eigh•teen**
eigh•teen
eightteen : **eigh•teen**
ekeing : **ek•ing**
ek•ing
elabarate : **e•lab•or•ate**
e•lab•o•rate
elaphant : **el•e•phant**
elemant : **el•e•ment**
elementary :
    el•e•men•ta•ry
el•e•ment
el•e•men•ta•ry
el•e•phant
elete : **elite**
eligibal : **el•i•gi•ble**
eligibel : **el•i•gi•ble**
el•i•gi•ble
elipse : **el•lipse**
e•lite
el•lipse
el•o•quence
eloquense : **el•o•quence**
embarass : **em•bar•rass**
embarras : **em•bar•rass**
em•bar•rass

em•bas•sy
embasy
embattelment :
    em•bat•tle•ment
em•bat•tle•ment
embattlment :
    em•bat•tle•ment
emergancy :
    e•mer•gen•cy
e•mer•gen•cy
em•i•grant (one who
    goes); **im•mi•grant**
    (one who comes)
eminant : **em•i•nent**
em•i•nent
emmersion : **im•mer•sion**
emolate : **im•mo•late**
emperer : **em•per•or**
em•per•or
enabel : **en•able**
en•able
enfeable : **en•fee•ble**
enfeebel : **en•fee•ble**
en•fee•ble
eniquity : **in•iq•ui•ty**
ennobel : **en•no•ble**
en•no•ble
enoble : **en•no•ble**
ensomnia : **in•som•nia**
enstallment :
    in•stall•ment
entireley : **en•tire•ly**
en•tire•ly
en•trance

entrence : **en•trance**
entricate : **in•tri•cate**
enviroment :
   en•vi•ron•ment
en•vi•ron•ment
e•qual•ly
equaly : **e•qual•ly**
equiped : **e•quipped**
equipmant : **e•quip•ment**
e•quip•ment
e•quipped
erchin : **ur•chin**
ern : **urn**
esayist : **es•say•ist**
esential : **es•sen•tial**
especialley : **es•pe•cial•ly**
es•pe•cial•ly
especialy : **es•pe•cial•ly**
espreso : **es•pres•so**
es•pres•so
essayest : **es•say•ist**
es•say•ist
es•sen•tial
es•thet•ic; aes•thet•ic
eth•i•cal
ethicle : **eth•i•cal**
e•ven•tu•al•ly
eventualy : **e•ven•tu•al•ly**
Eu•cha•rist
Eucherist : **Eu•cha•rist**
eufamism : **eu•phe•mism**
eulagy : **eu•lo•gy**
euligy : **eu•lo•gy**
eu•lo•gy

eunach : **eu•nuch**
eu•nuch
euphamism :
   eu•phe•mism
eu•phe•mism
euphimism :
   eu•phe•mism
eu•pho•ria
eu•tha•na•sia
euthenasia : **eu•tha•na•sia**
euthinasia : **eu•tha•na•sia**
euvre : **oeu•vre**
eve•ning
evning : **eve•ning**
ewe (female•sheep); **yew**
   (tree); **you** (pronoun)
exagerate : **ex•ag•ger•ate**
ex•ag•ger•ate
excead : **ex•ceed**
ex•ceed
excelence : **ex•cel•lence**
ex•cel•lence
ex•cept (not including);
   ac•cept (receive)
ex•cep•tion•al•ly
exceptionaly :
   ex•cep•tion•al•ly
ex•hil•a•rate
exhilerate : **ex•hil•a•rate**
exhilirate : **ex•hil•a•rate**
existance : **ex•is•tence**
ex•is•tence
experiance : **ex•pe•ri•ence**
ex•pe•ri•ence

experimant :
   ex•per•i•ment
ex•per•i•ment
ex•pla•na•tion
explination :
   ex•pla•na•tion
expresion : **ex•pres•sion**
ex•pres•sion

expresso : **espres•so**
exstasy : **ec•sta•sy**
extraordenary :
   ex•traor•di•nary
ex•traor•di•nary
extrordinary :
   ex•traor•di•nary

Ff

fa•ble
fab•ric
fabricait : **fab•ri•cate**
fab•ri•cate
fabrick : **fab•ric**
faceshus : **fa•ce•tious**
fa•ce•tious
facileties : **fa•cil•i•ties**
fa•cil•i•ties
facilitys : **fa•cil•i•ties**
facinating : **fas•ci•na•ting**
facsimale : **fac•sim•i•le**
fac•sim•i•le
factsimile : **fac•sim•i•le**
faible : **fa•ble**
faign : **feign**
falacy : **fal•la•cy**
fal•la•cy
fallecy : **fal•la•cy**
fallic : **phal•lic**
fam•i•lies
familys : **fam•i•lies**
famlies : **fam•i•lies**
fanciar : **fan•ci•er**
fan•ci•er
fan•ci•ful

fancifull : **fan•ci•ful**
fancyful : **fan•ci•ful**
fancyier : **fan•ci•er**
fan•ta•sy
farmacy : **phar•ma•cy**
far•sight•ed
farsited : **far•sight•ed**
fascinateing :
    fas•ci•na•ting
fas•ci•na•ting
fasetious : **fa•ce•tious**
fasinating : **fas•ci•na•ting**
fa•tal•is•ti•cal•ly
fatalisticaly :
    fa•tal•is•ti•cal•ly
fa•tal•ly
fataly : **fa•tal•ly**
fatelistically :
    fa•tal•is•ti•cal•ly
fatelly : **fa•tal•ly**
faxsimile : **fac•sim•i•le**
fa•ce•tious
fearfilly : **fear•ful•ly**
fear•ful•ly
fearfuly : **fear•ful•ly**

fearlesness :
   fear•less•ness
fear•less•ness
feasability : **fea•si•bil•i•ty**
feasable : **fea•si•ble**
feasant : **phea•sant**
feasibilaty : **fea•si•bil•i•ty**
fea•si•bil•i•ty
fea•si•ble
feazibility : **fea•si•bil•i•ty**
febrary : **Feb•ru•ar•y**
Febrary : **Feb•ru•ar•y**
Feb•ru•ar•y
Februery : **Feb•ru•ar•y**
Feburary : **Feb•ru•ar•y**
February : **Feb•ru•ar•y**
feign
feonix : **phoe•nix**
fe•ro•cious•ness
ferocousness :
   fe•ro•cious•ness
ferosiousness :
   fe•ro•cious•ness
fertilaztion :
   fer•til•iza•tion
fertilezation :
   fer•til•iza•tion
fer•til•iza•tion
feu•dal•ism
ficticious : **fic•ti•tious**
ficticous : **fic•ti•tious**
fic•ti•tious
fidality : **fi•del•i•ty**
fidelaty : **fi•del•i•ty**

fi•del•i•ty
filabuster : **fil•i•bus•ter**
fil•i•bus•ter
fillabuster : **fil•i•bus•ter**
fi•nal•ly
finaly : **fi•nal•ly**
financeally : **fi•nan•cial•ly**
financer : **fi•nan•cier**
fi•nan•cial•ly
financialy : **fi•nan•cial•ly**
fi•nan•cier
fineally : **fi•nal•ly**
fision : **fis•sion**
fis•sion
fis•sure
fisure : **fis•sure**
fition : **fis•sion**
flab•ber•gast
flabergast : **flab•ber•gast**
flem : **phlegm**
fluancy : **flu•en•cy**
flu•en•cy
fluincy : **flu•en•cy**
flu•o•res•cence
fluoresence :
   flu•o•res•cence
fluoresense :
   flu•o•res•cence
fluresence :
   flu•o•res•cence
fo•li•age
folliage : **fo•liage**
fonetic : **pho•ne•tic**
for•eign

forein : **for•eign**
foren : **for•eign**
formaly : **for•mal•ly**
formerlly : **for•mer•ly**
for•mer•ly
forth : (forward)
fourth (number)
fourtean : **four•teen**
four•teen
fourth
fracsionalize :
   frac•tion•al•ize
fractionalise :
   frac•tion•al•ize
frac•tion•al•ize
frend : **friend**
friend
frontearsman :
   fron•tiers•man
fronteresman :
   fron•tiers•man

fron•tiers•man
fru•gal•ly
frugaly : **fru•gal•ly**
fudalism : **feu•dal•ism**
fudelism : **feu•dal•ism**
fuge : **fugue**
fugue
ful•fill
ful•fill•ment
fulfilment : **ful•fill•ment**
fullfill : **ful•fill**
fullfilmant : **ful•fill•ment**
funaral : **fu•ner•al**
fu•ner•al
fungas : **fun•gus**
fun•gus
fun•ni•ness
funnyness : **fun•ni•ness**
furnature : **fur•ni•ture**
fur•ni•ture

Gg

gad•get
gadiness : **gaud•i•ness**
gadjet : **gad•get**
gage : **gauge**
gaget : **gad•get**
gaiaty : **gai•ety**
gai•ety
gai•ly
ga•lac•tic
galantry : **gal•lant•ry**
galatic : **ga•lac•tic**
gal•ax•y
galery : **gal•lery**
gal•lant•ry
gallary : **gal•lery**
gallaxy : **gal•axy**
gallentry : **gal•lant•ry**
gal•lery
gal•lop
gallup : **gal•lop**
galop : **gal•lop**
galvanise : **gal•va•nize**
gal•va•nize
galvenise : **gal•va•nize**
gambet : **gam•bit**
gam•bit

gamebit : **gam•bit**
gangreen : **gan•grene**
gan•grene
garanium : **ge•ra•ni•um**
garison : **gar•ri•son**
garmant : **gar•ment**
gar•ment
garralous : **gar•ru•lous**
garralus : **gar•ru•lous**
garrason : **gar•ri•son**
gar•ri•son
gar•ru•lous
garulous : **gar•ru•lous**
gas•eous•ness
gasousness :
   gas•eous•ness
gastraintestinal :
   gas•tro•in•tes•ti•nal
gastrointestenal :
   gas•tro•in•tes•ti•nal
gas•tro•in•tes•ti•nal
gauche (tactless);
   gouache (painting)
gaudeness : **gaud•i•ness**
gaud•i•ness
gauge

gauntily : **jaun•ti•ly**
gaushe : **gauche** (tactless);
  gouache (painting)
gavelin : **jav•e•lin**
gayety : **gai•ety**
gayly : **gai•ly**
gealous : **jeal•ous**
gel•a•tin
gellatin : **gel•a•tin**
genarous : **gen•er•ous**
ge•ne•al•o•gist
geneologist :
  ge•ne•al•o•gist
gen•er•al•iza•tion
generasity : **gen•er•os•i•ty**
generelization :
  gen•er•al•iza•tion
gen•er•os•i•ty
gen•er•ous
generus : **gen•er•ous**
genteal : **gen•teel**
gen•teel
gentele : **gen•teel**
geraniam : **ge•ra•ni•um**
ge•ra•ni•um
geremiad : **jer•e•mi•ad**
germacidal :
  ger•mi•cid•al
germanal : **ger•mi•nal**
germecital : **ger•mi•cid•al**
ger•mi•cid•al
ger•mi•nal
ges•tic•u•la•tion
geurilla : **guer•ril•la**

gibbarish : **gib•ber•ish**
gib•ber•ish
gib•bon
gib•bous
gibbun : **gib•bon**
gibbus : **gib•bous**
giberish : **gib•ber•ish**
gibon : **gib•bon**
gibous : **gib•bous**
gi•gan•tic
gig•gle
gigle : **gig•gle**
gimick : **gim•mick**
gim•mick
gimnasium :
  gym•na•si•um
ginecologist :
  gy•ne•col•o•gist
girafe : **gi•raffe**
gi•raffe
gizard : **giz•zard**
giz•zard
gizzerd : **giz•zard**
glaceir : **gla•cier**
gla•cier
glasher : **gla•cier**
gloat
glote : **gloat**
glutonous : **glut•ton•ous**
glut•ton•ous
gluttonus : **glut•ton•ous**
gnat
goashe : **gauche** (tactless);
  gouache (painting)

gonerrhea : **gon•or•rhea**
gonorea : **gon•or•rhea**
gonorhea : **gon•or•rhea**
gon•or•rhea
goorou : **gu•ru**
gor•geous
gorgious : **gor•geous**
gorgous : **gor•geous**
gorilla : **guer•ril•la**
gorrilla : **guer•ril•la**
gouache (painting);
   gauche (tactless)
gouche : **gauche** (tactless);
   gouache (painting)
gragarious : **gre•gar•i•ous**
grandaddy :
   grand•dad•dy
grand•dad•dy
granddady :
   grand•dad•dy
grates : **gra•tis**

gra•tis
gratouity : **gra•tu•ity**
gratuety : **gra•tu•ity**
gra•tu•ity
gregareous : **gre•gar•i•ous**
gre•gar•i•ous
grotesk : **gro•tesque**
grotesqeu : **gro•tesque**
gro•tesque
guerrila : **guer•ril•la**
guer•ril•la
guide•line
guidline : **guide•line**
gu•ru
gymnasiam :
   gyn•na•si•um
gym•na•si•um
gynacologist :
   gy•ne•col•o•gist
gy•ne•col•o•gist

Hh

hab•er•dash•er

habirdasher :
   hab•er•dash•er

ha•bit•u•ate

habituete : ha•bit•u•ate

haceinda : ha•ci•en•da

hacianda : ha•ci•en•da

ha•ci•en•da

hack•ney

hackny : hack•ney

hag•gle

hagle : hag•gle

hai•ku

hail (weather; greeting);
   hale (healthy)

hainous : hei•nous

hakney : hack•ney

hale (healthy); hail
   (weather; greeting)

hal•lu•ci•nate

halocaust : ho•lo•caust

halucinate : hal•lu•ci•nate

hamer : ham•mer

ham•mer

ham•mock

hammuck : ham•mock

hamock : ham•mock

hamorrhage :
   hem•or•rhage

hand•i•cap

handycap : hand•i•cap

hand•ker•chief

handkirchief :
   hand•ker•chief

hang•glide

hanglide : hang•glide

hapen : hap•pen

hapening : hap•pen•ing

hap•haz•ard

haphazird : hap•haz•ard

hapily : hap•pi•ly

hap•pen

hap•pen•ing

happenning : hap•pen•ing

hap•pi•ly

happin : hap•pen

hap•pi•ness

happining : hap•pen•ing

happly : hap•pi•ly

hap•py

happyness : hap•pi•ness

hapy : hap•py

harang : **ha•rangue**
ha•rangue
ha•rass
harber : **har•bor**
har•bor; har•bour
har•bour; har•bor
harbur : **har•bor;**
  har•bour
haring : **her•ring**
haringbone :
  her•ring•bone
harmoneius :
  har•mo•ni•ous
har•mo•ni•ous
harmonyus :
  har•mo•ni•ous
harpsechord :
  harp•si•chord
harp•si•chord
harpsicord :
  harp•si•chord
harrass : **ha•rass**
hart (male deer): **heart**
  (organ)
haynous : **hei•nous**
head•dress
head•light
headlite : **head•light**
headress : **head•dress**
health•ful
health•full : **health•ful**
hearce : **hearse**
hear•ing
hearring : **hear•ing**

hearse
heart
hearth•stone
heartstone : **hearth•stone**
heck•le
hedge
hege : **hedge**
hedlight : **head•light**
height•en
hei•nous
heinus : **hei•nous**
hekle : **heck•le**
heliam : **he•li•um**
he•li•um
hellthful : **health•ful**
hemorage : **hem•or•rhage**
hemorhoid :
  hem•or•rhoid
hemoroid : **hem•or•rhoid**
hemorrage :
  hem•or•rhage
hem•or•rhage
hem•or•rhoid
hemorroid : **hem•or•rhoid**
hendrance : **hin•drance**
heraditary : **he•red•i•tary**
herange : **ha•rangue**
herass : **ha•rass**
heratage : **her•i•tage**
heredatary : **he•red•i•tary**
he•red•i•tary
hereing : **hear•ing**
heretage : **her•i•tage**
hering : **her•ring**

heringbone :
  her•ring•bone
her•i•tage
her•ring
her•ring•bone
herse : **hearse**
hiarchy : **hi•er•ar•chy**
hic•cup
hickup : **hic•cup**
hicup : **hic•cup**
hidraulic : **hy•drau•lic**
hieghton : **height•en**
hi•er•ar•chy
hi•er•o•glyph•ic
higene : **hy•giene**
highten : **height•en**
higiene : **hy•giene**
hikou : **hai•ku**
hi•ly : **jai•a•lai**
hin•drance
hindrence : **hin•drance**
hiphenate : **hy•phen•ate**
hipie : **hip•pie**
hipnosis : **hyp•no•sis**
hipochondria :
  hy•po•chon•dria
hipocracy : **hy•poc•ri•sy**
hipopotamus :
  hip•po•pot•a•mus
hipoppatamus :
  hip•po•pot•a•mus
hip•pie
hippopatomus :
  hip•po•pot•a•mus

hip•po•pot•a•mus
hippy : **hip•pie**
hiroglyphic :
  hi•er•o•glyph•ic
histeria : **hys•te•ria**
historiagrapher :
  his•to•ri•og•ra•pher
his•to•ri•og•ra•pher
historyagrapher :
  his•to•ri•og•ra•pher
hoard (amass)
hollocost : **ho•lo•caust**
ho•lo•caust
holocost : **ho•lo•caust**
homaginous :
  ho•mo•ge•neous
homeapathy :
  ho•me•op•a•thy
homecide : **hom•i•cide**
homeastasis :
  ho•meo•sta•sis
ho•me•op•a•thy
ho•meo•sta•sis
hom•i•cide
homoganus :
  ho•mo•ge•neous
ho•mo•ge•neous
homogenus :
  ho•mo•ge•neous
horde (mob): **hoard**
  (amass)
hortaculture :
  hor•ti•cul•ture

horteculture :
   hor•ti•cul•ture
hor•ti•cul•ture
humanetarian :
   hu•man•i•tar•i•an
hu•man•i•tar•i•an
hu•mon•gous
humongus : **hu•mon•gous**
humungus : **hu•mon•gous**
huricane : **hur•ri•cane**
hurracane : **hur•ri•cane**
hur•ri•cane
hurrycane : **hur•ri•cane**
hydralic : **hy•drau•lic**
hy•drau•lic
hyerarchy : **hi•er•ar•chy**

hygeine : **hy•giene**
hy•giene
hypacracy : **hy•poc•ri•sy**
hyphanate : **hy•phen•ate**
hy•phen•ate
hypnoses : **hyp•no•sis**
hyp•no•sis
hypochandria :
   hy•po•chon•dria
hy•po•chon•dria
hy•poc•ri•sy
hyroglyphic :
   hi•er•o•glyph•ic
hystaria : **hys•te•ria**
hys•te•ria
hi•ly : jai•a•lai

Ii

i•am•bic
icey : ic•y
ich•thy•ol•o•gist
ic•i•cle
icie : icy
i•con
i•con•o•clasm
iconoklasm :
   icon•o•clasm
icthiologist :
   ich•thy•ol•o•gist
ic•y
icycle : ici•cle
idelness : idle•ness
ide•o•log•i•cal
idiological :
   ide•o•log•i•cal
idiosincrasy :
   id•io•syn•cra•sy
idiosyncracy :
   id•io•syn•cra•sy
id•io•syn•cra•sy
i•dle•ness
iembic : i•am•bic
igalitarian :
   e•gal•i•tar•i•an

ignishun : ig•ni•tion
ig•ni•tion
ig•no•rance
ignorence : ig•no•rance
ikonoclasm :
   i•con•o•clasm
ikthyologist :
   ich•thy•ol•o•gist
ilaborate : e•lab•o•rate
ilboding : ill•bod•ing
ilegality : il•le•gal•i•ty
ilegitimate :
   il•le•git•i•mate
ilhumored : ill•hu•mored
ilicit : il•lic•it
illaborate : e•lab•o•rate
illastrate : il•lus•trate
ill•bod•ing
il•le•gal•i•ty
illegitemate :
   il•le•git•i•mate
il•le•git•i•mate
ill•hu•mored
il•lic•it
il•log•i•cal
il•lu•mi•nate

il•lu•sion
il•lu•so•ry
il•lus•trate
ilogical : il•log•i•cal
iluminate : il•lu•mi•nate
ilusion : illusion
ilusory : il•lu•so•ry
ilustrate : il•lus•trate
imaculate : im•mac•u•late
imagineation :
   i•mag•i•na•tion
i•mag•i•na•tion
im•be•cil•i•ty
imbesility : im•be•cil•i•ty
imbicility : im•be•cil•i•ty
imbrew : im•brue
imbru : im•brue
im•brue
imcomepetence :
   in•com•pe•tence
imediacy : im•me•di•a•cy
imensely : im•mense•ly
imersion : im•mer•sion
imigrant : im•mi•grant
im•mac•u•late
immaculet :
   im•mac•u•late
immagrant : im•mi•grant
immansly : im•mense•ly
im•me•di•a•cy
im•mense•ly
im•mer•sion
immidiacy :
   im•me•di•a•cy

im•mi•grant (come);
   em•i•grant (go)
immobel : immobile
im•mo•bile
im•mo•late
im•mor•al
immpressible :
   im•press•ible
im•mune
imobile : im•mo•bile
imolate : im•mo•late
imoral : im•mor•al
impacience : im•pa•tience
im•pal•pa•ble
impalpible :
   im•pal•pa•ble
impanderable :
   im•pon•der•a•ble
impasable : im•pass•able;
   im•pas•si•ble
impasive : im•pas•sive
im•pass•able;
   im•pas•si•ble
impassibility :
   im•pos•si•bil•i•ty
im•pas•si•ble ;
   im•pass•able
im•pas•sive
im•pa•tience
impatus : im•pe•tus
im•peach•ment
impedement :
   im•ped•i•ment
im•ped•i•ment

impeechment :
  im•peach•ment
imperal : **im•per•il**
im•pe•ri•al•ist
im•per•il
im•per•me•able
impermisible :
  im•per•mis•si•ble
im•per•mis•si•ble
impersanate :
  im•per•son•ate
im•per•son•ate
impertarbable :
  im•per•turb•able
imperterbable :
  im•per•turb•able
im•per•turb•able
im•pe•tus
impirialist :
  im•pe•ri•al•ist
impirmeable :
  im•per•me•able
impitus : **im•pe•tus**
implasability :
  im•plau•si•bil•i•ty
implausability :
  im•plau•si•bil•i•ty
im•plau•si•bil•i•ty
im•pon•der•a•ble
imposibility :
  im•pos•si•bil•i•ty
im•pos•si•bil•i•ty
im•pov•er•ish

impovirish :
  im•pov•er•ish
impractacable :
  im•prac•ti•ca•ble
im•prac•ti•ca•ble
impresible :
  im•press•i•ble
impresionable :
  im•pres•sion•able
impresionism :
  im•pres•sion•ism
impresive : **im•pres•sive**
im•press•ible
im•pres•sion•able
im•pres•sion•ism
im•pres•sive
impudance : **im•pu•dence**
im•pu•dence
imune : **im•mune**
inabriation :
  in•e•bri•a•tion
inaccesible :
  in•ac•ces•si•ble
in•ac•ces•si•ble
in•ac•cu•ra•cy
in•ac•cu•rate
inacessible :
  in•ac•ces•si•ble
inacuracy : **in•ac•cu•ra•cy**
inacurate : **in•ac•cu•rate**
inadmisible :
  in•ad•mis•si•ble
inadmissable :
  in•ad•mis•si•ble

in•ad•mis•si•ble
in•an•i•mate
inaniment:•in•an•i•mate
inaminate : in•an•i•mate
in•ap•pro•pri•ate
inapropriate :
  in•ap•pro•pri•ate
inaquity : in•iq•ui•ty
inassential : in•es•sen•tial
inate : in•nate
in•aug•ur•al
incalcuelable :
  in•cal•cu•la•ble
in•cal•cu•la•ble
incansistency :
  in•con•sis•ten•cy
incence : in•cense
in•cense
incesant : in•ces•sant
in•ces•sant
incinsere : in•sin•cere
inclamency :
  in•clem•en•cy
in•clem•en•cy
incomepressible :
  in•com•press•ible
incompatence :
  in•com•pe•tence
in•com•pe•tence
incompresible :
  in•com•press•ible
in•com•press•ible
in•con•sis•ten•cy
in•con•ve•nience

inconvinience :
  in•con•ve•nience
incorigible :
  in•cor•ri•gi•ble
in•cor•ri•gi•ble
in•cor•rupt
incorupt : in•cor•rupt
incular : in•su•lar
in•cur•able
incureable : in•cur•able
indefenceable :
  in•de•fen•si•ble
indefencible :
  in•de•fen•si•ble
in•de•fen•si•ble
in•dict•ment
inditement : in•dict•ment
indoctranation :
  in•doc•tri•na•tion
in•doc•tri•na•tion
indubatable :
  in•du•bi•ta•ble
in•du•bi•ta•ble
in•e•bri•a•tion
inefable : in•ef•fa•ble
inefectual : in•ef•fec•tu•al
in•ef•fa•ble
in•ef•fec•tu•al
inersha : in•er•tia
in•er•tia
inesential : in•es•sen•tial
in•es•sen•tial
inexastible :
  in•ex•haust•ible

inexaustible :
  in•ex•haust•ible
in•ex•haust•ible
infedelity : **in•fi•del•i•ty**
infidality : **in•fi•del•i•ty**
in•fi•del•i•ty
influantial : **in•flu•en•tial**
in•flu•en•tial
in•iq•ui•ty
inirtia : **in•er•tia**
in•nate
innoble : **en•no•ble**
in•noc•u•ous
innoquous : **in•noc•u•ous**
in•nu•en•do
inocuous : **in•noc•u•ous**
inogural : **in•aug•ur•al**
inpatience : **im•pa•tience**
inqueitude : **in•qui•e•tude**
in•qui•e•tude
insafficient :
  in•suf•fi•cient
insence : **in•cense**
insencere : **in•sin•cere**
insense : **in•cense**
in•sep•a•ra•ble
inseperable :
  in•sep•a•ra•ble
insergence : **in•sur•gence**
in•sin•cere
insolance : **in•so•lence**
in•so•lence
insolense : **in•so•lence**
insomia : **in•som•nia**

in•som•nia
in•stall•ment
instalment : **in•stall•ment**
insuferable :
  in•suf•fer•able
insuffarable :
  in•suf•fer•able
in•suf•fer•able
in•suf•fi•cient
insuficient :
  in•suf•fi•cient
in•su•lar
insurgance : **in•sur•gence**
in•sur•gence
insuscaptible :
  in•sus•cep•ti•ble
in•sus•cep•ti•ble
insuseptible :
  in•sus•cep•ti•ble
intergect : **in•ter•ject**
in•ter•ject
in•ter•lo•cu•tion
intermiten :
  in•ter•mit•tent
in•ter•mit•tent
interprid : **in•trep•id**
interacial : **in•ter•rac•ial**
in•ter•rac•ial
intracate : **in•tri•cate**
intrapid : **in•trep•id**
in•trep•id
in•tri•cate
inuando : **in•nu•en•do**
inuendo : **in•nu•en•do**

invinceable : **in•vin•ci•ble**
in•vin•ci•ble
ionazation : **ion•iza•tion**
ion•iza•tion
irational : **ir•ra•tio•nal**
iredeemable :
    ir•re•deem•able
iretrievable :
    ir•re•triev•able
irevocable :
    ir•rev•o•ca•ble
iridecence : **ir•i•des•cence**
ir•i•des•cence
iritable : **ir•ri•ta•ble**
iritant : **ir•ri•tant**
irratable : **ir•ri•ta•ble**
irratant : **ir•ri•tant**

ir•ra•tio•nal
irredeamable :
    ir•re•deem•able
ir•re•deem•able
irretreivable :
    ir•re•triev•able
ir•re•triev•able
ir•rev•o•ca•ble
ir•ri•ta•ble
ir•ri•tant
irrivocable :
    ir•rev•o•ca•ble
isicle : **ic•i•cle**
itenerary : **i•tin•er•ary**
itinarary : **i•tin•er•ary**
i•tin•er•ary

Jj

jack•al
jackel : **jack•al**
jackhamer :
 jack•ham•mer
jack•ham•mer
jagar : **jag•uar**
jag•uar
jai•alai
jamberee : **jam•bo•ree**
jambore : **jam•bo•ree**
jam•bo•ree
janator : **jan•i•tor**
jandice : **jaun•dice**
janetor : **jan•i•tor**
jan•i•tor
jantily : **jaun•ti•ly**
jaun•dice
jaun•ti•ly
javalin : **jav•e•lin**
jav•e•lin
jawndice : **jaun•dice**
jeal•ous
jellatin : **gel•a•tin**
jelous : **jeal•ous**
jenteel : **gen•teel**
jeop•ar•dize

jeoperdize : **jeop•ar•dize**
jeopirdize : **jeop•ar•dize**
jeramiad : **jer•e•mi•ad**
jer•e•mi•ad
jeremyad : **jer•e•mi•ad**
jerminal : **ger•mi•nal**
jesticulation :
 ges•tic•u•la•tion
jetison : **jet•ti•son**
jetteson : **jet•ti•son**
jet•ti•son
jew•el•er
jewler : **jew•el•er**
jextepose : **jux•ta•pose**
jibberish : **gib•ber•ish**
jigantic : **gi•gan•tic**
jig•gle
jigle : **jig•gle**
jili : **jai•a•lai**
jimnasium :
 gym•na•si•um
jiraffe : **gi•raffe**
jocuelar : **joc•u•lar**
joc•u•lar
joger : **jog•ger**
jog•ger

joqular : **joc•u•lar**
joury : **ju•ry**
jouvenile : **ju•ve•nile**
jo•vial
joviel : **jo•vial**
jubalant : **ju•bi•lant**
jubelant : **ju•bi•lant**
ju•bi•lant
jug•gle
jugle : **jug•gle**
jurasdiction :
   ju•ris•dic•tion
jurasprudence :

   ju•ris•pru•dence
juresdiction :
   ju•ris•dic•tion
juresprudence :
   ju•ris•pru•dence
ju•ris•dic•tion
ju•ris•pru•dence
ju•ry
juvanile : **ju•ve•nile**
ju•ve•nile
jux•ta•pose
juxtepose : **jux•ta•pose**

Kk

ka•bob; ke•bob; ke•bab
kaelin : ka•o•lin
kaiak : kay•ak
ka•lei•do•scope
kalidascope :
　　ka•lei•do•scope
kaliedoscope :
　　ka•lei•do•scope
kamekaze : ka•mi•ka•ze
ka•mi•ka•ze
kamikazee : ka•mi•ka•ze
kan•ga•roo
kangeroo : kan•ga•roo
ka•o•lin
kapout : ka•put
ka•put
kar•at; car•at
ka•ra•te
karosene : ker•o•sene
karot : kar•at; car•at
karrat : kar•at; car•at
kawanza : kwan•za
kay•ak
kean : keen
keen
keln : kiln

kemical : chem•i•cal
kenel : ken•nel
kennal : ken•nel
ken•nel
ker•a•tin
keretin : ker•a•tin
ker•nel
ker•o•sene
ketledrum : ket•tle•drum
ketteldrum : ket•tle•drum
ket•tle•drum
kichen : kitch•en
kid•nap•er; kid•nap•per
kid•nap•per; kid•nap•er
kid•ney
kidny : kid•ney
killogram : ki•lo•gram
kiln
ki•lo•gram
kinamatic : ki•ne•mat•ic
kinatic : ki•net•ic
kindal : kin•dle
kin•der•gar•ten
kindharted :
　　kind•heart•ed
kind•heart•ed

kindirgarten :
   kin•der•gar•ten
kin•dle
ki•ne•mat•ic
ki•net•ic
kirnel : **ker•nel**
kiropractor :
   chi•ro•prac•tor
kitch•en
kiten : **kit•ten**
kittan : **kit•ten**
kit•ten
kleptamaniac :
   klep•to•ma•ni•ac
klep•to•ma•ni•ac
knap•sack
knav•ery
knavry : **knav•ery**
knead
kneal : **kneel**
kneed : **knead**

kneel
knick•ers
knight
knite : **knight**
knit•wear
knock•out
knoledgeable :
   knowl•edge•able
knowl•edge•able
knowlegable :
   knowl•edge•able
knuckal : **knuck•le**
knuck•le
koral : **cho•ral**
korate : **ka•ra•te**
ko•sher
kripton : **kryp•ton**
kryp•ton
Ku•wait; Kuweit
kuwate : **Kuwait**
kwan•za

LI

labal : **la•bel**
labaled : **la•beled**
la•bel
la•beled
labelled : **la•beled**
laber : **la•bor**
labido : **li•bi•do**
labirinth : **lab•y•rinth**
la•bor
lab•o•ra•to•ry
laboreously :
    la•bo•ri•ous•ly
laboretory :
    lab•o•ra•to•ry
la•bo•ri•ous•ly
labratory : **lab•o•ra•to•ry**
labrinth : **lab•y•rinth**
lab•y•rinth
lacadaisical :
    lack•a•dai•si•cal
lacarate : **lac•er•ate**
lac•er•ate
lack•a•dai•si•cal
lackadaysical :
    lack•a•dai•si•cal
lacktate : **lac•tate**

lac•quer
lacqur : **lac•quer**
lacross : **la•crosse**
la•crosse
lac•tate
lad•der
lader : **lad•der**
lagar : **la•ger**
la•ger
lagger : **la•ger**
lagician : **lo•gi•cian**
lagitimate : **le•git•i•mate**
la•goon
lagoun : **la•goon**
laiser : **la•ser**
laisez•fare : **lais•sez•faire**
lais•sez•faire
lamanate : **lam•i•nate**
lamantation :
    lam•en•ta•tion
lamenate : **lam•i•nate**
lam•en•ta•tion
lam•i•nate
lamintation :
    lam•en•ta•tion
lampost : **lamp•post**

lamp•post
lander : **laun•der**
langage : **lan•guage**
languad : **lan•guid**
lan•guage
langued : **lan•guid**
languege : **lan•guage**
lan•guid
lantil : **len•til**
lapce : **lapse**
lapse
laquer : **lac•quer**
larangitis : **lar•yn•gi•tis**
laranx : **lar•ynx**
larcanous : **lar•ce•nous**
larcany : **lar•ce•ny**
lar•ce•nous
lar•ce•ny
lareate : **lau•re•ate**
larengitis : **lar•yn•gi•tis**
laringitis : **lar•yn•gi•tis**
larinx : **lar•ynx**
larseny : **lar•ce•ny**
larsinous : **lar•ce•nous**
lar•yn•gi•tis
lar•ynx
la•sa•gna
lasana : **la•sa•gna**
lasegna : **la•sa•gna**
la•ser
lasir : **la•ser**
latancy : **la•ten•cy**
latatude : **lat•i•tude**
la•ten•cy

lat•er•al
latetude : **lat•i•tude**
latice : **lat•tice**
latincy : **la•ten•cy**
latiral : **lat•er•al**
lat•i•tude
latrean : **la•trine**
latrene : **la•trine**
la•trine
lattace : **lat•tice**
latteral : **lat•er•al**
lat•tice
laun•der
lau•re•ate
lauriate : **lau•re•ate**
lav•a•to•ry
lavetory : **lav•a•to•ry**
lavitory : **lav•a•to•ry**
lax•a•tive
laxetive : **lax•a•tive**
laysezfaire : **lais•sez• faire**
lazenge : **loz•enge**
lazer : **la•ser**
laziar : **la•zi•er**
la•zi•er
la•zi•ness
lazyer : **la•zi•er**
lazyness : **la•zi•ness**
leadan : **lead•en**
lead•en
leaprosy : **lep•ro•sy**
leapt
lease
leasion : **le•sion**

leason : **li•ai•son**
leasurely : **lei•sure•ly**
leatard : **le•o•tard**
leath•er
lecharous : **lech•er•ous**
lech•er•ous
lecrosse : **la•crosse**
ledan : **lead•en**
leden : **lead•en**
leese : **lease**
legable : **leg•i•ble**
leg•a•cy
legand : **leg•end**
legaslate : **leg•is•late**
legaslator : **leg•is•lator**
legecy : **leg•a•cy**
leg•end
legeslate : **leg•is•late**
legiannaire : **le•gion•naire**
leg•i•ble
legionaire : **le•gion•naire**
le•gion•naire
leg•is•late
leg•is•lator
legitamate : **le•git•i•mate**
le•git•i•mate
lei•sure•ly
lemen : **lem•on**
lemenade : **lem•on•ade**
lemmon : **lem•on**
lemmonade : **lem•on•ade**
lem•on
lem•on•ade
lemonaid : **lem•on•ade**

leneancy : **le•ni•en•cy**
lengthaning :
    length•en•ing
length•en•ing
lengthning : **length•en•ing**
leniancy : **le•ni•en•cy**
leniement : **lin•ea•ment**
le•ni•en•cy
lenin : **lin•en**
lental : **len•til**
lenthening : **length•en•ing**
len•til
le•o•tard
leperchaun : **lep•re•chaun**
leprechan : **lep•re•chaun**
lep•re•chaun
leprekaun : **lep•re•chaun**
leprichaun : **lep•re•chaun**
leprocy : **lep•ro•sy**
lep•ro•sy
lept : **leapt**
lesagne : **la•sa•gne**
les•bi•an
lesbien : **les•bi•an**
lesen : **less•en•**
    (to decrease)
le•sion
leson : **les•son•** (to read)
lessan : **less•en**
    (to decrease)
less•en• (to decrease)
les•son (to read)
lesurely : **lei•sure•ly**
leter : **let•ter**

le•thar•gic
lether : **leath•er**
leting : **let•ting**
lettar : **let•ter**
let•ter
let•ting
let•tuce
lettus : **let•tuce**
letuce : **let•tuce**
leu•ke•mia
leutenant : **lieu•ten•ant**
levarage : **le•ver•age**
levaty : **lev•i•ty**
le•ver•age
levety : **lev•i•ty**
le•vi•a•than
leviethan : **le•vi•a•than**
lev•i•ty
lewd
lexacon : **lex•i•con**
lex•i•con
lexycon : **lex•i•con**
lezbian : **les•bi•an**
li•a•ble
li•ai•son
liasen : **li•ai•son**
libal : **li•bel**
libaral : **lib•er•al**
libaration : **lib•er•a•tion**
libedo : **li•bi•do**
li•bel
lib•er•al
liberaries : **li•brar•ies**
lib•er•a•tion

li•bi•do
libiral : **lib•er•al**
libiration : **lib•er•a•tion**
li•brar•ies
librarys : **li•brar•ies**
libreries : **li•brar•ies**
li•cense
lickorice : **lic•o•rice**
lic•o•rice
licorise : **lic•o•rice**
lieable : **li•a•ble**
liesurely : **lei•sure•ly**
lieu•ten•ant
light
light•en•ing• (illuminate);
    light•ning (atmosphere)
light•ning (atmosphere);
    light•en•ing
    (illuminate)
ligitamate : **le•git•i•mate**
lik•a•ble
likeable : **lik•a•ble**
like•li•hood
likelyhood : **like•li•hood**
likor : **li•quor**
limarick : **lim•er•ick**
limarik : **lim•er•ick**
lim•er•ick
limosine : **lim•ou•sine**
lim•ou•sine
limph : **lymph**
linage : **lin•e•age**
linan : **lin•en**
lin•eage

lin•ea•ment
lin•en
lingist : **lin•guist**
lingthening :
 length•en•ing
lin•guist
liniage : **lin•eage**
liniament : **lin•ea•ment**
linnen : **lin•en**
linx : **lynx**
liposucktion :
 lip•o•suc•tion
lip•o•suc•tion
liqer : **li•queur** (flavored
 liquor); **li•quor**
 (alcohol)
liqor : **li•quor** (alcohol);
 li•queur (flavored
 liquor)
liquadate : **liq•ui•date**
liquedate : **liq•ui•date**
liquer : **li•queur** (flavored
 liquor); **li•quor**
 (alcohol)
li•queur (flavored liquor);
 li•quor (alcohol)
liq•ui•date
li•quor (alcohol);
 li•queur (flavored
 liquor)
lirical : **lyr•i•cal**
lisence : **li•cense**
lisense : **li•cense**
litagate : **lit•i•gate**

litaracy : **lit•er•acy**
litarature : **lit•er•a•ture**
lite : **light**
litening : **light•en•ing**
 (illuminate); **light•ning**
 (atmosphere)
lit•er•acy
lit•er•al•ly
literaly : **lit•er•al•ly**
lit•er•a•ture
litergy : **lit•ur•gy**
lithagraph : **lith•o•graph**
lithargic : **le•thar•gic**
lithegraph : **lith•o•graph**
lith•o•graph
lit•i•gate
litiracy : **lit•er•acy**
litirature : **lit•er•a•ture**
lit•ur•gy
liutenant : **lieu•ten•ant**
liveliast : **live•li•est**
live•li•est
liviathan : **le•vi•a•than**
log•a•rithm
logarythm : **log•a•rithm**
loged : **logged**
logerithm : **log•a•rithm**
logged
lo•gi•cian
logishan : **lo•gi•cian**
loneleness : **lone•li•ness**
lone•li•ness
longavity : **lon•gev•i•ty**
longevety : **lon•gev•i•ty**

lon•gev•i•ty
lonliness : **lone•li•ness**
losenge : **loz•enge**
lotery : **lot•tery**
lot•tery
loubricant : **lu•bri•cant**
loukemia : **leu•ke•mia**
louminance : **lu•mi•nance**
lov•a•ble
loveable : **lov•a•ble**
loy•al•ty
loyelty : **loy•al•ty**
lozange : **loz•enge**
loz•enge
lubracant : **lu•bri•cant**
lu•bri•cant
lucious : **lus•cious**
lude : **lewd**
lugage : **lug•gage**
lug•gage
lukemia : **leu•ke•mia**
lumanance : **lu•mi•nance**

lu•mi•nance
lu•na•cy
lunasy : **lu•na•cy**
luneacy : **lu•na•cy**
lus•cious
lushous : **lus•cious**
lusious : **lus•cious**
lutanant : **lieu•ten•ant**
lutenant : **lieu•ten•ant**
luxariance : **lux•u•ri•ance**
luxeriance : **lux•u•ri•ance**
luxries : **lux•u•ries**
lux•u•ri•ance
lux•u•ries
lyable : **li•a•ble**
lybel : **li•bel**
lymph
lynx
lyposuction :
    lip•o•suc•tion
lyracal : **lyr•i•cal**
lyr•i•cal

Mm

mac•a•ro•ni
mac•a•roon
macenry : ma•son•ry
macentosh : mac•in•tosh;
   mack•in•tosh
maceroni : mac•a•ro•ni
mach•i•na•tion
ma•chin•ery
machuration :
   mat•u•ra•tion
mac•in•tosh• :
   mack•in•tosh
mackaroni : mac•a•ro•ni
mackaroon : mac•a•roon
mackentosh :
   mac•in•tosh;
   mack•in•tosh
mackination :
   mach•i•na•tion
mack•in•tosh ;
   mac•in•tosh
ma•dam (singular);
   ma•dame (singular);
   mes•dames (plural)
ma•dame (singular);
   ma•dam (singular);

mes•dames (plural)
madamesele :
   ma•de•moi•selle
madamoiselle :
   ma•de•moi•selle
maddan : mad•den
mad•den
mademeselle :
   ma•de•moi•selle
ma•de•moi•selle
ma•de•moi•selle
   (singular);
   mes•de•moiselles
   (plural)
maden : mad•den
madula : me•dull•a
mael•strom
maem : maim
maentainable :
   main•tain•able
mae•stro
magestracy :
   mag•is•tra•cy
magget : mag•got
mag•got

mag•ic

mag•is•tra•cy

magnatism : **mag•ne•tism**

magneficient :
　mag•nif•i•cent

mag•ne•tism

mag•nif•i•cent

magority : **ma•jor•i•ty**

magot : **mag•got**

ma•hog•a•ny

mailstrom : **mael•strom**

maim

main•tain•able

maionnaise :
　may•on•naise

maistro : **mae•stro**

majic : **mag•ic**

majestracy :
　mag•is•tra•cy

ma•jor•i•ty

mak•able; make•able

make•able; mak•able

makeing : **mak•ing**

mak•ing

maladgusted :
　mal•ad•just•ed

mal•ad•just•ed

mal•aise

malaiz : **mal•aise**

ma•lar•ia

malase : **mal•aise**

malavolence :
　ma•lev•o•lence

maleability :
　mal•le•a•bil•i•ty

maledjusted :
　mal•ad•just•ed

malee : **me•lee**

malegnant : **ma•lig•nant**

maleria : **ma•lar•ia**

malestrom : **mael•strom**

malevalence :
　ma•lev•o•lence

ma•lev•o•lence

mal•fea•sance

malfeasence :
　mal•fea•sance

malfeesence :
　mal•fea•sance

malfesance :
　mal•fea•sance

ma•lig•nant

malivolence :
　ma•lev•o•lence

mal•lea•bil•i•ty

malliability :
　mal•le•a•bil•i•ty

mamal : **mam•mal**

mambrane : **mem•brane**

mame : **maim**

mam•mal

mammel : mam•mal

mam•moth

mamoth : **mam•moth**

mamouth : **mam•moth**

man•a•cle

manacurist :
   man•i•cur•ist
man•a•ge•ri•al
ma•nag•er•ie :
   me•nag•er•ie
manakin : **man•i•kin;**
   man•ne•quin
man•i•kin; man•ne•quin
mander : **maun•der**
manecle : **man•a•cle**
maned : **manned**
manegerial :
   man•a•ge•ri•al
manepulate :
   ma•nip•u•late
manered : **man•nered**
manetainable :
   main•tain•able
ma•neu•ver
manewer : **ma•nure**
manicle : **man•a•cle**
man•i•cur•ist
manigerial :
   man•a•ge•ri•al
ma•nip•u•late
maniqurist : **man•i•cur•ist**
manned
mannekin : **man•i•kin;**
   man•ne•quin
man•nered
manouver : **ma•neu•ver**
manslahter :
   man•slaugh•ter
man•slaugh•ter

manslauter :
   man•slaugh•ter
mansloughter :
   man•slaugh•ter
mansoon : **mon•soon**
mantor : **men•tor**
man•u•al
manuel : **man•u•al**
manuer : **ma•nure**
ma•nure
manuver : **ma•neu•ver**
marader : **ma•rau•der**
marage : **mi•rage**
maranate : **mar•i•nate**
mar•a•schi•no
marashino :
   mar•a•schi•no
ma•raud•er
mareachi : **ma•ri•a•chi**
marechino :
   mar•a•schi•no
marejuana : **mar•i•jua•na**
marenate : **mar•i•nate**
mar•ga•rine
mar•ga•ri•ta
margerine : **mar•ga•rine**
margirine : **mar•ga•rine**
marguerita : **mar•ga•ri•ta**
ma•ri•a•chi
mariachy : **ma•ri•a•chi**
mariage : **mar•riage**
maridian : **me•rid•i•an**
mariege : **mar•riage**
marihuana : **mar•i•jua•na**

mar•i•jua•na
mar•i•nate
maritorious :
   mer•i•to•ri•ous
markee : **mar•quee**
mar•ma•lade
marmelade :
   mar•ma•lade
marmilade : **mar•ma•lade**
maronic : **mo•ron•ic**
ma•roon
marow : **mar•row**
mar•quee
mar•riage
mar•row
marsh•mal•low
marshmellow :
   marsh•mal•low
marshmelo :
   marsh•mal•low
marsoupial : **mar•su•pi•al**
mar•su•pi•al
marsupiel : **mar•su•pi•al**
martir : **mar•tyr**
mar•tyr
marune : **ma•roon**
masachism : **mas•och•ism**
masacre : **mas•sa•cre**
masage : **mas•sage**
masanry : **ma•son•ry**
mas•cara
mascueline : **mas•cu•line**
mas•cu•line
masechism : **mas•och•ism**

maseuse : **mas•seuse**
maskara : **mas•car•a**
maskerade :
   mas•quer•ade
maskuline : **mas•cu•line**
mas•och•ism
masoleam : **mau•so•le•um**
masoleum :
   mau•so•le•um
ma•son•ry
masqarade :
   mas•quer•ade
mas•quer•ade
mas•sa•cre
mas•sage
mas•seuse
massicre : **mas•sa•cre**
massuse : **mas•seuse**
masterbation :
   mas•tur•ba•tion
mastirbation :
   mas•tur•ba•tion
mas•tur•ba•tion
masuse : **mas•seuse**
matanay : **mat•i•nee**
matenay : **mat•i•nee**
matereal : **ma•te•ri•al**
ma•te•ri•al
math•e•mat•ics
mathematics :
   math•e•mat•ics
maticulous :
   me•tic•u•lous
mat•i•nee

matirial : **ma•te•ri•al**
matracide : **ma•tri•cide**
matramonial :
  mat•ri•mo•nial
matramony :
  mat•ri•mo•ny
matrarchy : **ma•tri•ar•chy**
matrecide : **ma•tri•cide**
matremonial :
  mat•ri•mo•nial
matremony :
  mat•ri•mo•ny
matress : **mat•tress**
ma•tri•ar•chy
ma•tri•cide
mat•ri•mo•nial
mat•ri•mo•ny
mat•tress
mat•u•ra•tion
matureation :
  mat•u•ra•tion
matureity : **ma•tu•ri•ty**
ma•tu•ri•ty
maun•der
mau•so•le•um
maxamum : **max•i•mum**
maxemum : **max•i•mum**
max•i•mum
mayannaise :
  may•on•naise
maylee : **me•lee**
may•on•naise
mea•ger
me•an•der

meanial : **me•nial**
meas•ure
meateor : **me•te•or**
meateorite : **me•te•or•ite**
mechinery : **ma•chin•ery**
medacinal : **me•dic•i•nal**
medalion : **me•dal•lion**
me•dal•lion
medatate : **med•i•tate**
med•dle
medeaval : **me•di•eval**
medecinal : **me•dic•i•nal**
medeival : **me•di•eval**
medetate : **med•i•tate**
me•dic•i•nal
me•di•eval
mediocar : **me•di•o•cre**
me•di•o•cre
med•i•tate
medle : **med•dle**
medoulla : **me•dul•la**
me•dul•la
meeger : **mea•ger**
meger : **mea•ger**
mehogany : **ma•hog•a•ny**
mei•o•sis
mejority : **ma•jor•i•ty**
melan : **mel•on**
mel•an•choly
melankoly : **mel•an•choly**
melaria : **ma•lar•ia**
me•lee
meleu : **mi•lieu**
melignant : **ma•lig•nant**

mellodic : **me•lod•ic**

mellon : **mel•on**

mel•low

me•lod•ic

mel•on

melow : **mel•low**

memair : **mem•oir**

membrain : **mem•brane**

mem•brane

mem•oir

memonic : **mne•mon•ic**

mem•o•ra•bil•i•a

memrabilia :
   mem•o•ra•bil•i•a

memrar : **mem•oir**

memrobilia :
   mem•o•ra•bil•i•a

me•nag•er•ie

me•nial

meniel : **me•nial**

men•tor

merage : **mi•rage**

meratricious :
   mer•e•tri•cious

merauder : **ma•raud•er**

mercanary : **mer•ce•nary**

mer•ce•nary

meretrecious :
   mer•e•tri•cious

mer•e•tri•cious

me•rid•i•an

merily : **mer•ri•ly**

mer•i•to•ri•ous

merraly : **mer•ri•ly**

mer•ri•ly

merritorious :
   mer•i•to•ri•ous

mes•dames (plural);
   ma•dam (singular);
   ma•dame (singular)

mes•de•moi•selles
   (plural);
   ma•de•moi•selle
   (singular)

meshinery : **ma•chin•ery**

mesure : **meas•ure**

metabalic : **met•a•bol•ic**

met•a•bol•ic

metalic : **me•tal•lic**

metallac : **me•tal•lic**

me•tal•lic

metallion : **me•dal•lion**

metearite : **me•te•or•ite**

metebolic : **met•a•bol•ic**

meteculous :
   me•tic•u•lous

me•te•or

me•te•or•ite

me•tic•u•lous

metior : **me•te•or**

metiorite : **me•te•or•ite**

mettle : **med•dle**

mezanine : **mez•za•nine**

mezenine : **mez•za•nine**

mez•za•nine

mezzenine : **mez•za•nine**

miander : **me•an•der**

micosis : **my•co•sis**

micrafiche : **mi•cro•fiche**
mi•cro•cosm
microfeche : **mi•cro•fiche**
mi•cro•fiche
microfish : **mi•cro•fiche**
microkosm : **mi•cro•cosm**
miday : **mid•day**
mid•day
midg•et
migget : **midg•et**
mi•graine
migrane : **mi•graine**
milage : **mile•age**
milameter : **mil•li•me•ter**
milannium :
    mil•len•ni•um
milatancy : **mil•i•tan•cy**
milatarize : **mil•i•ta•rize**
mile•age
milenium : **mil•len•ni•um**
milennium :
    mil•len•ni•um
miletancy : **mil•i•tan•cy**
miletarize : **mil•i•ta•rize**
mileu : **mi•lieu**
milianaire : **mil•lion•aire**
mi•lieu
milimeter : **mil•li•me•ter**
milionaire : **mil•lion•aire**
mil•i•tan•cy
mil•i•ta•rize
milk•i•ness
milkyness : **milk•i•ness**
millameter : **mil•li•me•ter**

millannium :
    mil•len•ni•um
millenium :
    mil•len•ni•um
mil•len•ni•um
mil•li•me•ter
mil•lion•aire
millionnaire :
    mil•lion•aire
mimacry : **mim•ic•ry**
mim•e•o•graph
mi•me•sis
mim•ic•ry
mimiograph :
    mim•e•o•graph
minamal : **min•i•mal**
minascule : **min•is•cule;**
    mi•nus•cule
min•i•mal
min•is•cule; mi•nus•cule
mi•nus•cule; min•is•cule
miopic : **my•o•pic**
miosis : **mei•o•sis**
mi•rage
mirauder : **ma•raud•er**
mircenary : **mer•ce•nary**
miriad : **myr•i•ad**
miridian : **me•rid•i•an**
miror : **mir•ror**
mirrage : **mi•rage**
mir•ror
mirtle : **myr•tle**
misal : **mis•sal** (book)
misaliance :
    mis•al•li•ance

mis•al•li•ance
mis•an•thrope
misapprahend :
   mis•ap•pre•hend
mis•ap•pre•hend
mis•ap•pro•pri•ate
misaprehend :
   mis•ap•pre•hend
misapropriate :
   mis•ap•pro•pri•ate
miscanstrue :
   mis•con•strue
miscariage :
   mis•car•riage
mis•car•riage
mischavous :
   mis•chie•vous
mischevous :
   mis•chie•vous
mis•chie•vous
mis•con•strue
mis•cre•ant
miscriant : mis•cre•ant
miscunstrue :
   mis•con•strue
misdameanor :
   mis•de•mean•or
mis•de•mean•or
misdemenor :
   mis•de•mean•or
misenthrope :
   mis•an•thrope
mi•ser
miserabel : mis•er•a•ble

mis•er•a•ble
mis•guid•ance
misguideance :
   mis•guid•ance
misile : mis•sile (weapon)
misinthrope :
   mis•an•thrope
mispell : mis•spell
misprononciation :
   mis•pro•nun•ci•a•tion
mis•pro•nun•ci•a•tion
misrable : mis•er•a•ble
mis•sal (book)
mis•sile (weapon)
misspel : mis•spell
mis•spell
missusage : mis•us•age
mistery : mys•tery
mistic : mys•tic
mistro : mae•stro
mis•us•age
misuseage : mis•us•age
mith : myth
mithology : my•thol•o•gy
mitoesis : mi•to•sis
mi•to•sis
mittan : mit•ten
mit•ten
mizer : mi•ser
mne•mon•ic
mnimonic : mne•mon•ic
mobeal : mo•bile
mo•bile
mocassin : moc•ca•sin

moc•ca•sin
moccassin : **moc•ca•sin**
modafier : **mod•i•fi•er**
mo•dal (of a mode):
  mod•el (set plan)
modalate : **mod•u•late**
modefier : **mod•i•fi•er**
mod•el (set plan) : **mod•al**
  (of a mode)
mod•i•fi•er
mod•u•late
mohogany : **ma•hog•a•ny**
molases : **mo•las•ses**
mo•las•ses
molification :
  mol•li•fi•ca•tion
mollafication :
  mol•li•fi•ca•tion
mollasses : **mo•las•ses**
mol•li•fi•ca•tion
momantarily :
  mo•men•tari•ly
momantum :
  mo•men•tum
mo•men•tari•ly
mo•men•tum
monachrome :
  mon•o•chrome
monagamy :
  mo•nog•a•my
monagram : **mon•o•gram**
monalog : **mon•o•logue** ;
  mono•log
mon•ar•chism

monarkism :
  mon•ar•chism
mon•as•tery
monatary : **mon•e•tary**
monatize : **mon•e•tize**
monegram : **mon•o•gram**
monestery : **mon•as•tery**
mon•e•tary
mon•e•tize
mongral : **mon•grel**
mon•grel
monichrome :
  mon•o•chrome
monistery : **mon•as•tery**
monitary : **mon•e•tary**
monitize : **mon•e•tize**
mon•o•chrome
monocrome :
  mon•o•chrome
mon•o•gram
mo•nog•a•my
monogomy :
  mo•nog•a•my
mon•o•log : **mon•o•logue**
mon•o•logue : **mon•o•log**
monosillable :
  mon•o•syl•la•ble
monosylable :
  mon•o•syl•la•ble
mon•o•syl•la•ble
monotheasm :
  mon•o•the•ism
mon•o•the•ism
mon•soon

morg : **morgue**
morgage : **mort•gage**
morgue
morner : **mourn•er**
mo•ron•ic
mort•gage
mosaleum :
   mau•so•le•um
moskue : **mosque**
mosque
moteef : **mo•tif**
mo•tif
moto : **mot•to**
mot•to
mourn•er
mous : **mousse** (food);
   mouse (rodent)
mouse (rodent); **mousse**
   (food)
mousse (food); **mouse**
   (rodent)
mov•a•bil•i•ty
mov•a•ble ; move•a•ble
moveability :
   mov•a•bil•i•ty
move•a•ble : mov•a•ble
muck•rak•er
mucle : **mus•cle**
   (body•tissue)
mu•cous• (slimy); **mu•cus**
   (secretion)
mu•cus (secretion);
   mu•cous (slimy)
mud•di•ness

mudiness : **mud•di•ness**
muecus : **mu•cous**
   (slimy); **mu•cus**
   (secretion)
muffan : **muf•fin**
muf•fin
mufin : **muf•fin**
muger : **mug•ger**
mug•ger
mukracker : **muck•rak•er**
mulato : **mu•lat•to**
mu•lat•to
mullatto : **mu•lat•to**
multatude : **mul•ti•tude**
multetude : **mul•ti•tude**
mul•ti•tude
mumer : **mum•mer**
mumify : **mum•mi•fy**
mum•mer
mum•mi•fy
mum•my
mumy : **mum•my**
mu•ral•ist
murealist : **mu•ral•ist**
musaum : **mu•se•um**
mus•cle (body tissue);
   mus•sel (mollusk)
musel : **mus•sel**
   (mollusk); **mus•cle**
   (body tissue)
musle : **mus•cle** (body
   tissue); **mus•sel**
   (mollusk)

mus•sel (mollusk);
　　mus•cle (body•tissue)
mutan : **mut•ton**
muteaneer : **mu•ti•neer**
mu•ti•neer
muton : **mut•ton**
mut•ton
mu•tu•al•ly
mutualy : **mu•tu•al•ly**
muzle : **muz•zle**
muz•zle
my•co•sis

mygraine : **mi•graine**
mymesis : **mi•me•sis**
my•o•pic
myosis : **mei•o•sis**
myr•i•ad
myr•tle
mystary : **mys•tery**
mys•tery
mys•tic
myth
mythalogy : **my•thol•o•gy**
my•thol•o•gy

Nn

nacturnal : **noc•tur•nal**

naeve : **na•ive**

naevity : **na•ive•té;
na•ive•ty**

naghtily : **naugh•ti•ly**

na•ive

na•ive•té; na•ive•ty

namable : **name•a•ble**

name•a•ble

nameble : **name•a•ble**

name•ly

namly : **name•ly**

nan•ny

nany : **nan•ny**

naping : **nap•ping**

nap•ping

napsack : **knap•sack**

naration : **nar•ra•tion**

narcalepsy : **nar•co•lep•sy**

narcisism : **nar•cis•sism**

nar•cis•sism

nar•co•lep•sy

nar•ra•tion

narsicism : **nar•cis•sism**

na•sal

nasea : **nau•se•a**

nasel : **na•sal**

naseous : **nau•seous**

nastalgia : **nos•tal•gia**

nat : **gnat**

natavism : **na•tiv•ism**

natevism : **na•tiv•ism**

natical : **nau•ti•cal**

na•tiv•ism

naugh•ti•ly

nauhtily : **naugh•ti•ly**

nau•sea

nau•seous

nautacal : **nau•ti•cal**

nau•ti•cal

na•val

navel : **na•val**

navery : **knav•ery**

navice : **nov•ice**

nead : **knead**

neadle : **nee•dle**

neal : **kneel**

neaprene : **neo•prene**

neccessary : **nec•ess•ary**

necesary : **nec•ess•ary**

nec•ess•ary

necissary : **nec•ess•ary**

neck•er•chief

necralogist :
 ne•crol•o•gist

necramancy :
 nec•ro•man•cy

necrapolis : ne•crop•o•lis

necremancy :
 nec•ro•man•cy

ne•crol•o•gist

nec•ro•man•cy

ne•crop•o•lis

nee•dle

neel : kneel

neghbor : neigh•bor

neglagence : neg•li•gence

neg•li•gence

neigh•bor

neihbor : neigh•bor

nekerchief : neck•er•chief

nemonic : mne•mon•ic

neoclasic : neo•clas•sic

ne•o•clas•sic

ne•on

ne•o•prene

nepatism : nep•o•tism

nep•o•tism

ner•vous

nervus : ner•vous

nestalgia : nos•tal•gia

neumonia : pneu•mon•ia

neu•ral

neuralogy : neu•rol•o•gy

neu•rol•o•gy

neu•ro•sis

neu•ter

neu•tral•iza•tion

neutrelization :
 neu•tral•iza•tion

newsleter : news•let•ter

news•let•ter

nialist : ni•hil•ist

nib•ble

nible : nib•ble

nicatine : nic•o•tine

nickalodeon :
 nick•el•ode•on

nick•el

nick•el•ode•on

nickers : knick•ers

nickilodeon :
 nick•el•ode•on

nickle : nick•el

nickotine : nic•o•tine

nic•o•tine

nigardly : nig•gard•ly

nig•gard•ly

niggerdly : nig•gard•ly

night (evening); knight
 (feudal warrior)

nihalist : ni•hil•ist

ni•hil•ist

nikelodeon :
 nick•el•ode•on

nimfomania :
 nym•pho•ma•nia

nimphomania :
 nym•pho•ma•nia

nioclassic : neo•clas•sic

nion : **ne•on**
niple : **nip•ple**
nip•ple
nitragen : **ni•tro•gen**
ni•tro•gen
nitwear : **knit•wear**
nockout : **knock•out**
noc•tur•nal
nomanee : **nom•i•nee**
no•men•cla•ture
nomenklature :
   no•men•cla•ture
nominclature :
   no•men•cla•ture
nom•i•nee
non•align•ment
nonalinement :
   non•align•ment
nonalinment :
   non•align•ment
non•cha•lance
nonchelance :
   non•cha•lance
noncomital :
   non•com•mit•tal
noncomittal :
   non•com•mit•tal
noncommital :
   non•com•mit•tal
non•com•mit•tal
nonsceduled :
   non•sched•uled
non•sched•uled
nonsuport : **non•sup•port**

non•sup•port
norcolepsy :
   nar•co•lep•sy
nor•mal•cy
normelcy : **nor•mal•cy**
noseness : **nos•i•ness**
nos•i•ness
nosious : **nox•ious**
nos•tal•gia
nostelgia : **nos•tal•gia**
nosyness : **nos•i•ness**
noteable : **no•ta•ble**
noteceable : **no•tice•able**
no•ta•ble
noticable : **no•tice•able**
no•tice•able
nouance : **nu•ance**
noucleus : **nu•cle•us**
noughtily : **naught•i•ly**
nousia : **nau•se•a**
nousious : **nau•seous**
novace : **nov•ice**
novelete : **nov•el•ette**
nov•el•ette
nov•ice
novilette : **nov•el•ette**
nowledgeable :
   know•ledge•able
nox•ious
nu•ance
nuckle : **knuck•le**
nucleas : **nu•cle•us**
nu•cle•us
nudasm : **nud•ism**

nudesm : **nud•ism**
nud•ism
nulafy : **nul•li•fy**
nulify : **nul•li•fy**
nullafy : **nul•li•fy**
nul•li•fy
num : **numb**
numb
numb•ness
numness : **numb•ness**
nunary : **nun•nery**
nunery : **nun•nery**
nunnary : **nun•nery**
nun•nery

nural : **neu•ral**
nurology : **neu•rol•og•y**
nurosis : **neu•ro•sis**
nuter : **neu•ter**
nutralization :
    neu•tral•iza•tion
nutreant : **nu•tri•ent**
nutriant : **nu•tri•ent**
nu•tri•ent
nuzle : **nuz•zle**
nuz•zle
nymfomania :
    nym•pho•ma•nia
nym•pho•ma•nia

Oo

oak•en
oakin : **oak•en**
oars•man
oases : **oa•sis**
oa•sis
obcene : **ob•scene**
ob•du•rate
obece : **o•bese**
obediance : **o•be•di•ence**
o•be•di•ence
o•bese
obidience : **o•be•di•ence**
obise : **o•bese**
objactive : **ob•jec•tive**
ob•jec•tive
oblagate : **ob•li•gate**
oblegate : **ob•li•gate**
obleige : **o•blige**
oblevion : **obliv•i•on**
ob•li•gate
o•blige
obliv•i•on
obnaxious : **ob•nox•ious**
ob•nox•ious
obo : **o•boe**
oboast : **o•bo•ist**

o•boe
o•bo•ist
obscean : **ob•scene**
ob•scene
obsene : **ob•scene**
ob•sess (to preoccupy)
obsess : ab•scess
   (inflammation)
obsoleat : **ob•so•lete**
obsoleet : **ob•so•lete**
ob•so•lete
ob•sta•cle
obstanacy : **ob•sti•na•cy**
obstecle : **ob•sta•cle**
obstenacy : **ob•sti•na•cy**
obsticle : **ob•sta•cle**
ob•sti•na•cy
ob•tain•able
obtaineable : **ob•tain•able**
obtaneable : **ob•tain•able**
obtous : **ob•tuse**
ob•tuse
oburate : **ob•du•rate**
ocasion : **oc•ca•sion**
ocassion : **oc•ca•sion**
oc•ca•sion

occassion : **oc•ca•sion**
oc•clude
oc•cu•pan•cy
occupency : **oc•cu•pan•cy**
occured : **oc•curred**
occurence : **oc•cur•rence**
oc•curred
oc•cur•rence
oceanagraphy :
  o•cean•og•ra•phy
o•cean•og•ra•phy
oceonography :
  o•cean•og•ra•phy
ocillate : **os•cil•late**
ocktet : **oc•tet**
oclude : **oc•clude**
oc•tag•o•nal
octapod : **oc•to•pod**
octapus : **oc•to•pus**
octegonal : **oc•tag•o•nal**
octepod : **oc•to•pod**
oc•tet
octigonal : **oc•tag•o•nal**
octit : **oc•tet**
oc•to•pod
oc•to•pus
ocuelar : **oc•u•lar**
oc•u•lar
ocupancy : **oc•cu•pan•cy**
ocured : **oc•curred**
ocurence : **oc•cur•rence**
ocurred : **oc•curred**
ocurrence : **oc•cur•rence**
odaty : **odd•i•ty**

oddaty : **odd•i•ty**
odd•i•ty
oddysey : **od•ys•sey**
oderous : **o•dor•ous**
odiam : **o•di•um**
odiem : **o•di•um**
odipal : **oed•i•pal**
odirous : **o•dor•ous**
odissey : **od•ys•sey**
odity : **odd•i•ty**
o•di•um
o•dor•ous
odorus : **o•dor•ous**
odurate : **ob•du•rate**
odysey : **od•ys•sey**
od•ys•sey
odyssy : **od•ys•sey**
oed•i•pal
oeu•vre
ofecious : **of•fi•cious**
ofence : **of•fense**
ofered : **of•fered**
oferred : **of•fered**
offanse : **of•fense**
offeciant : **of•fi•ci•ant**
offecious : **of•fi•cious**
offence : **of•fense**
of•fense
of•fered
offerred : **of•fered**
of•fi•ci•ant
of•fi•cious
oficiant : **of•fi•ci•ant**
oficious : **of•fi•cious**

ogal : **o•gle**
ogel : **o•gle**
o•gle
oint•ment
oister : **oys•ter**
oken : **oak•en**
olagarchy : **ol•i•gar•chy**
olagopoly : **ol•i•gop•o•ly**
o•le•ag•i•nous
oleajinous : **o•le•ag•i•nous**
olegarchy : **ol•i•gar•chy**
olegopoly : **ol•i•gop•o•ly**
o•le•o
oliaganous :
    o•le•ag•i•nous
oliaginous : **ole•ag•i•nous**
ol•i•gar•chy
ol•i•gop•o•ly
olio : **o•leo**
om•elet
omession : **o•mis•sion**
omision : **o•mis•sion**
o•mis•sion
omited : **o•mit•ted**
o•mit•ted
omlet : **om•elet**
ommited : **o•mit•ted**
omnabus : **om•ni•bus**
omnebus : **om•ni•bus**
om•ni•bus
onarous : **o•ner•ous**
o•ner•ous
onerus : **o•ner•ous**
onirous : **o•ner•ous**

onix : **on•yx**
on•o•ma•to•poe•ia
onomotopeia :
    on•o•ma•to•poe•ia
onomotopia :
    on•o•ma•to•poe•ia
on•yx
opake : **o•paque**
o•pal•es•cence
opalesense :
    o•pal•es•cence
opalessence :
    o•pal•es•cence
opaqe : **o•paque**
o•paque
opassum : **o•pos•sum**
opelescence :
    o•pal•es•cence
o•pi•ate
opiete : **o•pi•ate**
oponent : **op•po•nent**
oportune : **op•por•tune**
o•pos•sum
oposum : **o•pos•sum**
op•po•nent
op•por•tune
oppossum : **o•pos•sum**
oppresion : **op•pres•sion**
oppresive : **op•pres•sive**
op•pres•sion
op•pres•sive
opresion : **op•pres•sion**
opresive : **op•pres•sive**
opression : **op•pres•sion**

opressive : **op•pres•sive**
optamally : **op•ti•mal•ly**
optemally : **op•ti•mal•ly**
op•ti•mal•ly
optimaly : **op•ti•mal•ly**
op•tion•al•ly
optionaly : **op•tion•al•ly**
optionelly : **op•tion•al•ly**
oqular : **oc•u•lar**
orafice : **or•i•fice**
oragin : **or•i•gin**
or•al•ly
oraly : **or•al•ly**
or•ches•tra
orchistra : **or•ches•tra**
ordanance : **or•di•nance**
or•di•nance
orefice : **or•i•fice**
oregin : **or•i•gin**
orelly : **or•al•ly**
orfanage : **or•phan•age**
or•i•fice
or•i•gin
orkestra : **or•ches•tra**
or•phan•age
orphenage : **or•phan•age**
orphinage : **or•phan•age**
orsman : **oars•man**
oscilate : **os•cil•late**
os•cil•late
osilate : **os•cil•late**
osillate : **os•cil•late**
os•mo•sis
osteapath : **os•te•o•path**

ostensably : **os•ten•si•bly**
os•ten•si•bly
os•te•o•path
ostrach : **os•trich**
os•tra•cism
ostrech : **os•trich**
ostrecism : **os•tra•cism**
os•trich
ostricism : **os•tra•cism**
oter : **ot•ter**
ot•ter
ottir : **ot•ter**
out•ma•neu•ver
outmanuver :
    out•ma•neu•ver
outmenuver :
    out•ma•neu•ver
outraegous : **out•ra•geous**
out•ra•geous
outragous : **out•ra•geous**
ouvre : **oeu•vre**
ovuelate : **ov•u•late**
ov•u•late
oxemoron : **ox•y•mo•ron**
ox•en
oxigen : **ox•y•gen**
oxigin : **ox•y•gen**
oxigenate : **ox•y•gen•ate**
oxiginate : **ox•y•gen•ate**
oximoron : **ox•y•mo•ron**
oxin : **ox•en**
oxyganate : **ox•y•gen•ate**
ox•y•gen
oxygin : **ox•y•gen**

ox•y•mo•ron
ox•y•gen•ate

oys•ter
o•zone

Pp

pacient : **pa•tient**
pac•i•fist
pac•i•fy
pack•age
packige : **pack•age**
pa•gan
pag•eant
pageination :
   pag•i•na•tion
pagen : **pa•gan**
pagent : **pag•eant**
pagin : **pa•gan**
pag•i•na•tion
pagint : **pag•eant**
paible : **pay•a•ble**
pair (two things); **pare**
   (cut away); **pear** (fruit)
pais•ley
paisly : **pais•ley**
pa•ja•mas : py•ja•mas
pajammas : **pa•ja•mas** ;
   py•ja•mas
palacial : **pa•la•tial**
pal•at•able
pa•la•tial
palid : **pal•lid**

pallatable : **pal•at•able**
pal•lid
pal•lor
palor : **pal•lor**
pamflet : **pam•phlet**
pam•phlet
pamphlit : **pam•phlet**
pamplet : **pam•phlet**
panarama : **pan•o•ra•ma**
pan•cre•as
pancreus : **pan•cre•as**
pandamonium :
   pan•de•mo•ni•um
pan•de•mo•ni•um
pane (glass); **pain** (ache)
pan•eled : pan•elled
pan•elled : pan•eled
paper•mache : **pa•pier-
   mâ•ché**
pa•pier-mâ•ché
parabala : **pa•rab•o•la**
pa•rab•o•la
paradice : **par•a•dise**
par•a•digm
paradime : **par•a•digm**
par•a•dise

par•a•dox
parady : **par•o•dy**
parafernalia :
   par•a•pher•nalia
par•af•fin
parafin : **par•af•fin**
para•graph
par•a•keet
paralell : **par•al•lel**
paralisis : **pa•ral•y•sis**
par•al•lel
pa•ral•y•sis
par•a•noid
paraphanalia :
   par•a•pher•na•lia
paraphenalia :
   par•a•pher•na•lia
par•a•pher•na•lia
par•a•site
para•sol
par•cel
parden : **par•don**
par•don
pare (cut away); **pair**
   (two things); **pear**
   (fruit)
paridigm : **par•a•digm**
paridise : **par•a•dise**
pariffin : **par•af•fin**
parigraph : **par•a•graph**
parinoid : **par•a•noid**
par•ish (church
   community); **per•ish**
   (die)

parisite : **par•a•site**
parisol : **para•sol**
parlament : **par•lia•ment**
par•lance
parlence : **par•lance**
par•lia•ment
pa•ro•chi•al
parodox : **par•a•dox**
par•o•dy
parokeet : **par•a•keet**
parot : **par•rot**
paroxism : **par•ox•ysm**
parrallel : **par•al•lel**
parret : **par•rot**
parrit : **par•rot**
parrochial : **pa•ro•chi•al**
par•rot
parsel : **par•cel**
parseley : **pars•ley**
parshal : **par•tial**
pars•ley
parsly : **pars•ley**
partacle : **par•ti•cle**
par•tial
par•ti•cle
par•tridge
partrige : **par•tridge**
pasenger : **pas•sen•ger**
pasifist : **pac•i•fist**
pasion : **pas•sion**
pasley : **pais•ley**
pas•sen•ger
passify : **pac•i•fy**
passinger : **pas•sen•ger**

pas•sion
passon : **pas•sion**
pastery : **past•ry**
pas•teur•ize
pas•time
past•i•ness
pas•tor
pastorize : **pas•teur•ize**
past•ry
pasttime : **pas•time**
pastyness : **past•i•ness**
patern : **pat•tern**
pa•thet•ic
patholegy : **path•ol•o•gy**
path•ol•o•gy
pa•tience
patiense : **pa•tience**
pa•tient
patriarc : **pa•tri•arch**
pa•tri•arch
patrolium : **pe•tro•leum**
pa•tron•age
patronige : **pa•tron•age**
pat•tern
paun : **pawn**
pause (hesitate); **paws**
    (animal feet)
pavilian : **pa•vil•ion**
pa•vil•ion
pavillion : **pa•vil•ion**
pawn
paws (animal feet); **pause**
    (hesitate)
pay•a•ble

payible : **pay•a•ble**
peacan : **pe•can**
peace (calm); **piece**
    (portion)
peal (ring); **peel** (strip;
    rind)
pear (fruit); **pair**
    (two things); **pare**
    (cut away)
pear : **peer** (equal); **pier**
    (dock)
pearl (gem); **purl**
    (knitting)
peas•ant
peasent : **peas•ant**
peavish : **pee•vish**
pe•can
pe•cu•liar
peculier : **pe•cu•liar**
ped•a•gogue
pedagree : **ped•i•gree**
ped•al (foot lever);
    ped•dle (sell); **pet•al**
    (flower)
pedastel : **ped•es•tal**
ped•dle (sell); **ped•al**
    (foot lever); **pet•al**
    (flower)
ped•es•tal
pedestle : **ped•es•tal**
ped•i•gree
pedistal : **ped•es•tal**
peel (strip; rind); **peal**
    (ring)

peer (equal); pier (dock)
pee•vish
peice : peace (calm);
　piece (portion);
peir : peer (equal; peep);
　pier (dock)
peirce : pierce
pelet : pel•let
pel•let
pellit : pel•let
penacilin : pen•i•cil•lin
penacillan : pen•i•cil•lin
penacillin : pen•i•cil•lin
pen•al•ty
pen•ance
penanse : pen•ance
penatentiary :
　pen•i•ten•ti•ar•y
penatrate : pen•e•trate
pendalum : pen•du•lum
pendelum : pen•du•lum
pendulam : pen•du•lum
pen•du•lum
penecillen : pen•i•cil•lin
penence : pen•ance
pen•e•trate
penicilin : pen•i•cil•lin
pen•i•cil•lin
pen•in•su•la
penitance : pen•i•tence
penitant : pen•i•tent
pen•i•tence
penitenciary :
　pen•i•ten•ti•ar•y

pen•i•tent
pen•i•ten•tia•ry
penitrate : pen•e•trate
pen•ni•less
penninsula : pen•in•su•la
pennyless : pen•ni•less
penulty : pen•al•ty
peo•ple
percarious : pre•car•i•ous
per•ceive
perceptable :
　per•cep•ti•ble
per•cep•ti•ble
percieve : per•ceive
percipitation :
　pre•cip•i•ta•tion
per•emp•to•ry
perenial : pe•ren•ni•al
pe•ren•ni•al
perfectable : per•fect•ible
per•fect•ible
per•for•mance
performence :
　per•for•mance
periferal : pe•riph•er•al
pe•riph•er•al
per•ish (die); par•ish
　(church community)
permanant : per•ma•nent
per•ma•nent
per•me•able
permenant : per•ma•nent
permiable : per•me•able

permisible :
   per•mis•si•ble
permissable :
   per•mis•si•ble
per•mis•si•ble
per•ni•cious
pernitious : **per•ni•cious**
perogative :
   pre•rog•a•tive
perpandicular :
   per•pen•dic•u•lar
perpatrate : **per•pe•trate**
per•pen•dic•u•lar
perpendiculer :
   per•pen•dic•u•lar
per•pe•trate
perpitrate : **per•pe•trate**
perrenial : **pe•ren•ni•al**
perrogative :
   pre•rog•a•tive
persaverance :
   per•se•ver•ance
per•se•cute (oppress);
   pros•e•cute (legal)
perserverance :
   per•se•ver•ance
perserverence :
   per•se•ver•ance
per•se•ver•ance
perseverence :
   per•se•ver•ance
per•son•al (private);
   per•son•nel
   (employees)

personel : **per•son•al**
   (private); **per•son•nel**
   (employees)
pe•rson•nel (employees);
   per•son•al (private)
per•suade
persue : **pur•sue**
pertanent : **per•ti•nent**
perterb : **per•turb**
pertinant : **per•ti•nent**
per•ti•nent
per•turb
pesant : **peas•ant**
pesimism : **pes•si•mism**
pesimist : **pes•si•mist**
pes•si•mism
pes•si•mist
pestalence : **pes•ti•lence**
pestilance : **pes•ti•lence**
pes•ti•lence
pet•al (flower); **ped•al**
   (foot lever); **ped•dle**
   (sell)
pe•tro•leum
petrolium : **pe•tro•leum**
peuter : **pew•ter**
pew•ter
phalic : **phal•lic**
phal•lic
phar•ma•ceu•ti•cal
pharmacolagist :
   phar•ma•col•o•gist
phar•ma•col•o•gist

pharmacutical :
   phar•ma•ceu•ti•cal
phar•ma•cy
pharmecy : **phar•ma•cy**
pharmocologist :
   phar•ma•col•o•gist
pheas•ant
pheasent : **pheas•ant**
phenetic : **pho•ne•tic**
phenix : **phoe•nix**
phe•nom•e•nal
phe•nom•e•non
phenominal :
   phe•nom•e•nal
phenominon :
   phe•nom•e•non
pheonix : **phoe•nix**
phesant : **pheas•ant**
phillabuster : **fi•li•bus•ter**
philosiphy : **phi•los•o•phy**
phi•los•o•phy
phisics : **phys•ics**
phlegm
phlem : **phlegm**
phoe•nix
pho•ne•tic
phospherescent :
   phos•pho•res•cent
phospherous :
   phos•pho•rous (adj.);
   phos•phor•us (noun)
phosphorecent :
   phos•pho•res•cent

phosphoresant :
   phos•pho•res•cent
phos•pho•res•cent
phosphoresent :
   phos•pho•res•cent
phos•pho•rous (adj.);
   phos•phor•us (noun)
phos•phor•us (noun);
   phos•pho•rous (adj.)
photosinthesis :
   pho•to•syn•the•sis
pho•to•syn•the•sis
photosynthysis :
   pho•to•syn•the•sis
phys•ics
phy•sique
pianeer : **pi•o•neer**
piaza : **pi•az•za**
pi•az•za
piccalo : **pic•co•lo**
pic•co•lo
picolo : **pic•co•lo**
pid•gin (language);
   pi•geon (bird)
piece (portion); **peace**
   (calm)
pier (dock); **peer** (equal)
pierce
pi•geon (bird); **pid•gin**
   (language)
pigion : **pi•geon** (bird);
   pid•gin (language)
pigmy : **pyg•my**

pijamas : **pa•ja•mas;
py•ja•mas**
pil•low
pi•lot
pilow : **pil•low**
pinacle : **pin•na•cle**
pin•afore
pin•na•cle
pinnafore : **pin•afore**
pinnicle : **pin•na•cle**
pioneer :
   py•ro•ma•ni•ac
pirouet : **pir•ou•ette**
pir•ou•ette
pis•til (flower); **pis•tol**
  (gun)
pis•tol (gun); **pis•til**
  (flower)
pitaful : **pit•i•ful**
pit•e•ous
pithon : **py•thon**
pit•i•ful
pitious : **pit•e•ous**
piv•ot
pix•el
pixle : **pix•el**
placcid : **pla•cid**
pla•ce•bo
placibo : **pla•ce•bo**
pla•cid
plad : **plaid**
plage : **plague**
plagerism : **pla•gia•rism**

pla•gia•rism
plagierism : **pla•gia•rism**
plague
plaid
platatude : **plat•i•tude**
pla•teau
plat•i•tude
plausable : **plau•si•ble**
plau•si•ble
play•wright
playwrite : **play•wright**
pleas•ant
pleasent : **pleas•ant**
plea•sure
pledge
plege : **pledge**
plesant : **pleas•ant**
plesure : **plea•sure**
pli•ant
plient : **pli•ant**
plumb•er
plumb•ing
plummer : **plumb•er**
plumming : **plumb•ing**
pneu•mo•nia
pnuemonia : **pneu•mo•nia**
pnumonia : **pneu•mo•nia**
podiam : **po•di•um**
po•di•um
poi•gnant
poignent : **poi•gnant**
poinsetta : **poin•set•tia**
poin•set•tia
poisen : **poi•son**

poi•son
pol•ar
poler : po•lar
pol•i•cy
polinate : pol•li•nate
pollenate : pol•li•nate
pollicy : pol•i•cy
pol•li•nate
pomp•ous
pompus : pomp•ous
poperry : pot•pour•ri
popourri : pot•pour•ri
pop•u•lace (noun);
    pop•u•lous (adj.)
pop•u•lar
pop•u•lous (adj.);
    pop•u•lace (noun)
por•ce•lain
porcelin : por•ce•lain
poridge : por•ridge
por•ridge
porselin : por•ce•lain
por•ta•ble
portfoleo : port•fo•lio
port•fo•lio
portfollio : port•fo•lio
portible : por•ta•ble
por•trait
posative : pos•i•tive
posess : pos•sess
pos•i•tive
pos•se

pos•sess
postarity : pos•ter•i•ty
pos•ter•i•ty
po•ta•to
potatoe : po•ta•to
po•ta•toes
potatos : po•ta•toes
pot•pour•ri
prac•ti•cal
practicle : prac•ti•cal
prair : prayer
prai•rie
prarie : prai•rie
prayer
precareous : pre•car•i•ous
pre•car•i•ous
pre•cede (go before);
    pro•ceed (continue)
pre•ce•dent (that which
    comes before);
    pres•i•dent (head)
precense : pre•sence
pre•cious
precipace : prec•i•pice
prec•i•pice
pre•cip•i•ta•tion
predater : pred•a•tor
pred•a•tor
predecesor :
    pre•de•ces•sor
predecesser :
    pre•de•ces•sor
pre•de•ces•sor

predesessor :
pre•de•ces•sor
predicesser :
pre•de•ces•sor
predicessor :
pre•de•ces•sor
preditor : **pred•a•tor**
preferance : **pref•er•ence**
pref•er•ence
prefference : **pref•er•ence**
preg•nant
pregnent : **preg•nant**
preist : **priest**
prejudace : **prej•u•dice**
prej•u•dice
premeir : **pre•mier**
(chief); **pre•miere** (first
performance)
premeire : **pre•mier**
(chief); **pre•miere** (first
performance)
pre•mier (chief);
pre•miere (first
performance)
pre•miere (first
performance); **pre•mier**
(chief)
pre•oc•cu•pa•tion
preocuppation :
pre•oc•cu•pa•tion
prepair : **pre•pare**
pre•pare
preremptory :
per•emp•to•ry

prerequisate :
pre•req•ui•site
pre•req•ui•site
pre•rog•a•tive
prescence : **pres•ence**
(being present);
pre•sents (introduces);
pres•ents (gifts)
pres•ence (being present);
pre•sents (introduces);
pres•ents (gifts)
presense : **pres•ence**
(being present);
pre•sents (introduces);
pres•ents (gifts)
pre•sent•able
presentible : **pre•sent•able**
pre•sents (introduces);
pres•ence (being
present); **pres•ents**
(gifts)
pres•ents (gifts);
pres•ence (being
present); **pre•sents**
(introduces)
pres•i•dent (head);
prec•e•dent (that
which comes
before)
presious : **pre•cious**
prestege : **pres•tige**
pres•tige
pretzal : **pret•zel**
pret•zel

pre•vail
prevale : **pre•vail**
prier : **pri•or**
priest
primative : **prim•i•tive**
prim•i•tive
prin•ci•pal (chief);
　prin•ci•ple (moral rule)
prin•ci•ple (moral rule);
　prin•ci•pal (chief)
pri•or
prism
pri•va•cy
privalige : **priv•i•lege**
privecy : **pri•va•cy**
privelege : **priv•i•lege**
priviledge : **priv•i•lege**
priv•i•lege
prizm : **prism**
prob•a•ble
probible : **prob•a•ble**
pro•ceed (continue);
　pre•cede (go before)
procrastenate :
　pro•cras•ti•nate
pro•cras•ti•nate
proc•tor
prodegy : **prod•i•gy**
prod•ig•al
prodigel : **prod•i•gal**
prodigle : **prod•i•gal**
prod•i•gy
profesor : **pro•fes•sor**
professer : **pro•fes•sor**

pro•fes•sor
profoundity :
　pro•fun•di•ty
pro•fun•di•ty
prohibet : **pro•hib•it**
pro•hib•it
proliffic : **pro•lif•ic**
pro•lif•ic
prominant : **prom•i•nent**
prom•i•nent
pronounciation :
　pro•nun•ci•a•tion
pro•nun•ci•a•tion
pro•pa•gan•da
propeganda :
　pro•pa•gan•da
prophacy : **proph•e•cy**
(noun); **proph•e•sy**
(verb)
proph•e•cy (noun);
　proph•e•sy (verb)
proph•es•y (verb);
　proph•e•cy (noun)
pros•e•cute (legal);
　per•se•cute (oppress)
prosicute : **pros•e•cute**
　(legal); **per•se•cute**
　(oppress)
pseu•do•nym
psichiatry : **psy•chi•a•try**
psichology :
　psy•chol•o•gy
psy•chi•a•try
psy•chol•o•gy

psycology : **psy•chol•o•gy**

pteradactyl :
   pter•o•dac•tyl

pteridactyl :
   pter•o•dac•tyl

pterodactile :
   pter•o•dac•tyl

pter•o•dac•tyl

publicety : **pub•lic•i•ty**

pub•lic•i•ty

pulpet : **pul•pit**

pul•pit

pumace : **pum•ice**

pum•ice

pumkin : **pump•kin**

pummice : **pum•ice**

pump•kin

pup•pet

puppit : **pup•pet**

puraty : **pu•ri•ty**

purety : **pu•ri•ty**

pu•ri•ty

purl (knitting); **pearl**
   (gem)

pursuade : **per•suade**

pur•sue

pyg•my

py•ja•mas : pa•ja•mas

py•ro•ma•ni•ac

py•thon

Qq

qeue : **queue** (line); **cue**
  (signal; billiards)
quadrangel :
  quad•ran•gle
quad•ran•gle
quad•rant
qua•drat•ic
quadratick : **qua•drat•ic**
quadrent : **quad•rant**
quaf : **quaff**
quaff
quag•mire
quail
quaint
quaiver : **qua•ver**
qualafy : **qual•i•fy**
qualaty : **qual•i•ty**
quale : **quail**
qualefy : **qual•i•fy**
qual•i•fy
qual•i•ty
quallify : **qual•i•fy**
quallity : **qual•i•ty**
qualm
quam : **qualm**
quan•da•ry

quandery : **quan•da•ry**
quarel : **quar•rel**
quar•rel
quar•reled : **qua•rrelled**
quarrey : **quar•ry**
quar•ry
quart
quarts (plural of quart);
  quartz (mineral)
quartz (mineral); **quarts**
  (plural of quart)
qua•ver
quay
que : **queue** (line); **cue**
  (signal; billiards)
quean : **queen**
quear : **queer**
quea•sy
queazy : **quea•sy**
queeche : **quiche**
queen
queer
queery : **que•ry**
queesh : **quiche**
queesy : **quea•sy**
queralous : **quer•u•lous**

quer•u•lous
que•ry
questionaire :
   ques•tion•naire
ques•tion•naire
questionnare :
   ques•tion•naire
queue (line); **cue** (signal;
   billiards)
quey : **quay**
quibbel : **quib•ble**
quib•ble
quible : **quib•ble**
quiche
quiecent : **qui•es•cent**
quiescant : **qui•es•cent**
qui•es•cent
quiesent : **qui•es•cent**
quieshe : **quiche**
quil : **quill**
quill
quintescence :
   quin•tes•sence
quintesense :
   quin•tes•sence
quintessance :
   quin•tes•sence
quin•tes•sence
quip

quipp : **quip**
quire : **choir**
quisine : **cui•sine**
quite (entirely); **qui•et**
   (silent)
quiv•er
quivver : **quiv•er**
quiz
quizacal : **quiz•zi•cal**
quizical : **quiz•zi•cal**
quizz : **quiz**
quiz•zi•cal
quizzicle : **quiz•zi•cal**
qui•et (silent); **quite**
   (entirely)
quocient : **quo•tient**
quoff : **quaff**
quorem : **quo•rum**
quorrum : **quo•rum**
quort : **quart**
quo•rum
quo•ta
quot•able
quoteable : **quot•able**
quotiant : **quo•tient**
quo•tient
qwagmire : **quag•mire**
qwaint : **quaint**
qwota : **quo•ta**

Rr

rab•bi
rabi : **rab•bi**
rac•coon
rac•ism
rack•et
racoon : **rac•coon**
radacal : **rad•i•cal**
raddish : **rad•ish**
radeator : **ra•di•a•tor**
radeo : **ra•di•o**
ra•di•ance
radianse : **ra•di•ance**
radiater : **ra•di•a•tor**
ra•di•a•tor
rad•i•cal
radicle : **rad•i•cal**
radience : **ra•di•ance**
ra•di•o
rad•ish
rag•a•muf•fin
raggamuffin :
    rag•a•muf•fin
ragimuffin :
    rag•a•muf•fin
raign : **reign**
raindeer : **rein•deer**

raion : **ray•on**
raisen : **rai•sin**
rai•sin
raison : **rai•sin**
randam : **ran•dom**
randem : **ran•dom**
ran•dom
rap•id
rappid : **rap•id**
rapsody : **rhap•so•dy**
raquet : **rack•et**
rarety : **rar•i•ty**
rar•i•ty
rasberry : **rasp•ber•ry**
ras•cal
rascel : **ras•cal**
rascle : **ras•cal**
raser : **ra•zor**
rasin : **rai•sin**
rasism : **rac•ism**
rasor : **ra•zor**
rasp•ber•ry
ratrap : **rat•trap**
rattel : **rat•tle**
rat•tle
rat•trap

raveen : **ra•vine**
raveoli : **rav•i•o•li**
ra•vine
rav•i•o•li
ray•on
razberry : **rasp•ber•ry**
razer : **ra•zor**
ra•zor
reacter : **re•ac•tor**
re•ac•tor
read (book); **red** (color)
read (book); **reed** (plant)
re•ad•just
rea•dy
reajust : **re•ad•just**
reak : **reek** (stink); **wreak**
   (inflict)
realise (British) : **re•al•ize**
re•al•ize
realm
reap
reasen : **rea•son**
reasin : **rea•son**
rea•son
reath : **wreath** (noun);
   wreathe (verb)
reathe : **wreath** (noun);
   wreathe (verb)
rebelion : **re•bel•lion**
rebellian : **re•bel•lion**
re•bel•lion
re•but•tal
rebuttel : **re•but•tal**
rebuttle : **re•but•tal**

reccollection :
   rec•ol•lec•tion
reccommend :
   rec•om•mend
reccommend :
   rec•om•mend
reccurrance : **re•cur•rence**
reccurrence : **re•cur•rence**
re•cede
receed : **re•cede**
re•ceipt
receit : **re•ceipt**
receite : **re•ceipt**
re•ceive
re•cent (new); **re•sent** (be
   bitter)
recepie : **rec•i•pe**
re•cep•ta•cle
receptecle : **re•cep•ta•cle**
receptical : **re•cep•ta•cle**
recepticle : **re•cep•ta•cle**
receve : **re•ceive**
reciept : **re•ceipt**
recieve : **re•ceive**
rec•i•pe
recipiant : **re•cip•i•ent**
recipie : **rec•i•pe**
re•cip•i•ent
reciprical : **re•cip•ro•cal**
re•cip•ro•cal
reciprocle : **re•cip•ro•cal**
recipy : **rec•i•pe**
re•cit•al
recitel : **re•cit•al**

recitle : **re•cit•al**
reck•less
recognise (British) :
   rec•og•nize
rec•ol•lec•tion
recomend : **rec•om•mend**
rec•om•mend
recompence :
   rec•om•pense
rec•om•pense
re•con•cile
reconsile : **re•con•cile**
re•cruit
recrut : **re•cruit**
recurrance : **re•cur•rence**
re•cur•rence
recurrense : **re•cur•rence**
red (color); **read** (book)
reddress : **re•dress**
reddy : **rea•dy**
re•deem
redeme : **re•deem**
re•dress
re•duce
reduse : **re•duce**
reed (plant); **read** (book)
reek (stink); **wreak**
  (inflict)
re•en•try
reep : **reap**
re•ex•am•ine
re•fer
referance : **ref•er•ence**
ref•er•ee

ref•er•ence
referree : **ref•er•ee**
referrence : **ref•er•ence**
reffer : **re•fer**
refferee : **ref•er•ee**
refference : **ref•er•ence**
refridgerator :
   re•frig•er•a•tor
refrigerater :
   re•frig•er•a•tor
re•frig•er•a•tor
re•fus•al
refusel : **re•fus•al**
regada : **re•gat•ta**
regata : **re•gat•ta**
re•gat•ta
regeme : **re•gime**
regergitate :
   re•gur•gi•tate
reggatta : **re•gat•ta**
reggister : **reg•is•ter**
re•gime
reg•is•ter
reg•u•lar
reguler : **reg•u•lar**
re•gur•gi•tate
rehabilatate :
   re•ha•bil•i•tate
re•ha•bil•i•tate
rehabillitate :
   re•ha•bil•i•tate
re•hears•al
rehearsel : **re•hears•al**
rehearsle : **re•hears•al**
rehersal : **re•hears•al**

reign
reimberse : **re•im•burse**
re•im•burse
rein•deer
re•joice
rejoyce : **re•joice**
re•ju•ve•nate
rejuvinate : **re•ju•ve•nate**
reknown : **re•nown**
relagate : **rel•e•gate**
rel•a•tive
relavent : **rel•e•vant**
rel•e•gate
releive : **re•lieve**
rel•e•vant
releve : **re•lieve**
relevent : **rel•e•vant**
reliabal : **re•li•a•ble**
re•li•a•ble
re•li•ance
relience : **re•li•ance**
re•lieve
rel•ish
relitive : **rel•a•tive**
relize : **re•al•ize**
rellative : **rel•a•tive**
rellish : **rel•ish**
relm : **realm**
re•luc•tant
reluctent : **re•luc•tant**
relyance : **re•li•ance**
remady : **rem•e•dy**
re•main
remane : **re•main**

remanisce : **rem•i•nisce**
re•mark•able
remarkible : **re•mark•able**
remeadial : **re•me•di•al**
re•me•di•al
rem•e•dy
re•mem•brance
rememberance :
　re•mem•brance
remidial : **re•me•di•al**
remidy : **rem•e•dy**
reminice : **rem•i•nisce**
rem•i•nisce
reminise : **rem•i•nisce**
remitance : **re•mit•tance**
re•mit•tance
remittence : **re•mit•tance**
remmoval : **re•mov•al**
re•mov•al
removeal : **re•mov•al**
renagade : **ren•e•gade**
rench : **wrench**
rendavoo : **ren•dez•vous**
rendevous : **ren•dez•vous**
ren•dez•vous
ren•e•gade
re•new•al
renewel : **re•new•al**
renigade : **ren•e•gade**
renivate : **ren•o•vate**
re•nounce
renounse : **re•nounce**
ren•o•vate
re•nown

renownce : **re•nounce**

rentry : **re•en•try**

reoccurrence :
   re•cur•rence

re•pair

repairation : **rep•a•ra•tion**

rep•a•ra•tion

repare : **re•pair**

re•peal

repeatition : **rep•e•ti•tion**

repeel : **re•peal**

repelant : **re•pel•lent**

repelent : **re•pel•lent**

repellant : **re•pel•lent**

rep•el•lent

re•pen•tance

repentanse : **re•pen•tance**

repentence : **re•pen•tance**

rep•e•ti•tion

repitition : **rep•e•ti•tion**

repleca : **rep•li•ca**

rep•li•ca

repplica : **rep•li•ca**

reprahensible :
   rep•re•hen•si•ble

repramand : **rep•ri•mand**

reprehencible :
   rep•re•hen•si•ble

reprehensable :
   rep•re•hen•si•ble

rep•re•hen•si•ble

repreive : **re•prieve**

re•prieve

rep•ri•mand

re•pri•sal

re•proach

reproche : **re•proach**

repudeate : **re•pu•di•ate**

re•pu•di•ate

rep•u•ta•ble

reputible : **rep•u•ta•ble**

re•quit•al

requittal : **re•quit•al**

resadence : **res•i•dence**

resavoir : **res•er•voir**

re•scind

re•search

resede : **re•cede**

re•sent (be bitter) :
   re•cent (new)

reserch : **re•search**

res•er•voir

reservoire : **res•er•voir**

resevoir : **res•er•voir**

residance : **res•i•dence**

res•i•dence

re•sign

resiliant : **re•sil•ient**

re•sil•ient

resillient : **re•sil•ient**

resind : **re•scind**

resine : **re•sign**

resipe : **rec•i•pe**

re•sis•tance

resistanse : **re•sis•tance**

resistence : **re•sis•tance**

resital : **re•cit•al**

resivoire : **res•er•voir**

resorce : **re•source**
re•source
re•spect•able
respectible : **re•spect•able**
resperator : **res•pi•ra•tor**
respirater : **res•pi•ra•tor**
res•pi•ra•tor
responsable :
  re•spon•si•ble
re•spon•si•ble
ressurrect : **res•ur•rect**
ressurrect : **res•ur•rect**
restarant : **res•tau•rant**
restaraunt : **res•tau•rant**
res•tau•rant
restle : **wres•tle**
resurect : **res•ur•rect**
resurect : **res•ur•rect**
resurgance : **re•sur•gence**
re•sur•gence
res•ur•rect
resurrgence : **re•sur•gence**
retacence : **ret•i•cence**
re•tail
retale : **re•tail**
retch (vomit); wretch
  (miserable person)
retched : **wretch•ed**
reticance : **ret•i•cence**
ret•i•cence
reticense : **ret•i•cence**
ret•i•na
retisence : **ret•i•cence**
retoric : **rhet•o•ric**

retreive : **re•trieve**
retreve : **re•trieve**
re•trieve
rettail : **re•tail**
rettina : **ret•i•na**
revalation : **rev•e•la•tion**
revalry : **rev•el•ry**
re•veal
rev•eil•le
rev•el
rev•e•la•tion
revele : **re•veal**
revell : **rev•el**
rev•el•ry
reverant : **rev•er•ent**
rev•er•ent
rev•er•ie
re•ver•sal
reversel : **re•ver•sal**
revery : **rev•er•ie**
revilation : **rev•e•la•tion**
re•viv•al
revivel : **re•viv•al**
re•vo•ca•ble
revocible : **re•vo•ca•ble**
revrent : **rev•er•ent**
rexamine : **re•ex•am•ine**
rhapsady : **rhap•so•dy**
rhapsidy : **rhap•so•dy**
rhap•so•dy
rhet•o•ric
rhine•stone
rhi•noc•er•os

rhinocerous :
rhi•noc•er•os

rhinocerus : **rhi•noc•er•os**

rhinoseros : **rhi•noc•er•os**

rhithm : **rhythm**

rhombous : **rhom•bus**

rhom•bus

rhu•barb

rhyme

rhythem : **rhythm**

rhythm

rhythum : **rhythm**

rhythym : **rhythm**

ribben : **rib•bon**

ribbin : **rib•bon**

rib•bon

ribon : **rib•bon**

ricachay : **ric•o•chet**

rice

ricketty : **rick•ety**

rick•ety

rickity : **rick•ety**

ric•o•chet

ricoshay : **ric•o•chet**

ridacule : **rid•i•cule**

riddel : **rid•dle**

riddicule : **rid•i•cule**

riddiculous : **ri•dic•u•lous**

rid•dle

ridge

ridgid : **rig•id**

rid•i•cule

ri•dic•u•lous

ridiculus : **ri•dic•u•lous**

rie : **rye** (grain); **wry**
(ironic)

riet : **ri•ot** (disorder); **rite**
(custom)

rifel : **rif•fle**
(thumb through); **ri•fle**
(gun)

riffel : **rif•fle**
(thumb through); **ri•fle**
(gun)

rif•fle (thumb through);
ri•fle (gun)

ri•fle (gun); **rif•fle** (thumb
through)

rige : **ridge**

riged : **rig•id**

riger : **rig•ger** (boat);
rig•or (severity)

rig•ger (boat); **rig•or**
(severity)

riggid : **rig•id**

riggor : **rig•ger** (boat);
rig•or (severity)

right (correct; not left);
rite (custom); **write**
(mark paper)

righ•teous (upright);
ri•ot•ous (disorderly)

rightious : **righ•teous**

rig•id

rig•or (severity); **rig•ger**
(boat)

rime : **rhyme**

rince : **rinse**

rinestone : **rhine•stone**
rinkle : **wrin•kle**
rinoceros : **rhi•noc•er•os**
rinse
ri•ot
ri•ot•ous (disorderly);
   right•eous (upright)
rippel : **rip•ple**
rip•ple
rise : **rice**
riske : **ris•qué**
risquay : **ris•qué**
ris•qué
rist : **wrist**
rite (custom); **right**
   (correct; not left); **write**
   (mark paper)
riter : **writ•er**
rithe : **writhe**
rithm : **rhythm**
rithym : **rhythm**
ritious : **right•eous**
   (upright); **ri•ot•ous**
   (disorderly)
rittual : **rit•u•al**
rit•u•al
rituel : **rit•u•al**
ri•val
rivel : **ri•val**
rivle : **ri•val**
rivval : **ri•val**
roach
roast
robbin : **rob•in**

robbot : **ro•bot**
rob•in
ro•bot
robott : **ro•bot**
roche : **roach**
rock•et
rocketery : **rock•et•ry**
rock•et•ry
rockett : **rock•et**
rockit : **rock•et**
rodant : **ro•dent**
ro•dent
ro•deo
rodio : **ro•deo**
roge : **rogue**
rogue
role (actor's part); **roll**
   (bread; turn over)
roll (bread; turn over);
   role (actor's part)
ro•mance
romanse : **ro•mance**
rombus : **rhom•bus**
roomate : **room•mate**
room•mate
roste : **roast**
rotarry : **ro•ta•ry**
ro•ta•ry
rotery : **ro•ta•ry**
rough (not smooth); **ruff**
   (collar)
roy•al
royale : **roy•al**
royel : **roy•al**

rubarb : **rhu•barb**
ruff (collar); **rough**
  (not smooth)

rumer : **ru•mor**
ru•mor
rye (grain); **wry** (ironic)

Ss

sabatage : **sab•o•tage**
Sabath : **Sab•bath**
sabatical : **sab•bat•i•cal**
sabbatage : **sab•o•tage**
Sab•bath
sab•bat•i•cal
Sabbeth : **Sab•bath**
sabbotage : **sab•o•tage**
sabitage : **sab•o•tage**
sab•o•tage
sacarine : **sac•cha•rin**
  (sugar substitute);
  sac•cha•rine (too
  sweet)
saccarine : **sac•cha•rin**
  (sugar substitute);
  sac•cha•rine (too
  sweet)
sac•cha•rin (sugar
  substitute);
  sac•cha•rine (too
  sweet)
sachel : **satch•el**
sacrafice : **sac•ri•fice**
sac•ri•fice
sa•fa•ri

safarri : **sa•fa•ri**
saffari : **sa•fa•ri**
saffire : **sap•phire**
sail•er (boat); **sail•or**
  (person)
sail•or (person); **sail•er**
  (boat)
sal•ad
sal•a•man•der
sal•a•ry
salemander :
  sal•a•man•der
salid : **sal•ad**
salimander :
  sal•a•man•der
sallad : **sal•ad**
sallary : **sal•a•ry**
salled : **sal•ad**
salm•on
sal•vage
salvige : **sal•vage**
sammon : **salm•on**
sammurai : **sam•u•rai**
samon : **salm•on**
sam•u•rai
sanatary : **san•i•tary**

san•dal
sandel : **san•dal**
sandle : **san•dal**
sandwhich : **sand•wich**
sand•wich
sandwitch : **sand•wich**
sanety : **san•i•ty**
san•i•tary
san•i•ty
saphire : **sap•phire**
sap•phire
sar•casm
sarcazm : **sar•casm**
sareen : **se•rene**
sargent : **ser•geant**
sas•sa•fras
sassafrass : **sas•sa•fras**
satallite : **sat•el•lite**
satasfactory :
    sat•is•fac•to•ry
satch•el
satelite : **sat•el•lite**
sat•el•lite
sa•ti•ate
satieate : **sa•ti•ate**
sat•in
satisfactery :
    sat•is•fac•to•ry
sat•is•fac•to•ry
satté : **sau•té**
sattelite : **sat•el•lite**
satten : **sat•in**
sattilite : **sat•el•lite**
sattin : **sat•in**

sau•cer
sau•sage
sausege : **sau•sage**
sausser : **sau•cer**
saussige : **sau•sage**
sau•té
sav•age
savege : **sav•age**
savier : **sav•ior ; sav•iour**
savige : **sav•age**
sav•ior : sav•iour
saxaphone : **sax•o•phone**
saxiphone : **sax•o•phone**
sax•o•phone
scabard : **scab•bard**
scab•bard
scabberd : **scab•bard**
scabbord : **scab•bard**
scaf•fold
scafold : **scaf•fold**
scald
scalpal : **scal•pel**
scal•pel
scalple : **scal•pel**
scan•dal
scandel : **scan•dal**
scandle : **scan•dal**
scar•let
scarlett : **scar•let**
scarlit : **scar•let**
sceduel : **sched•ule**
scedule : **sched•ule**
sceme : **scheme**
sce•nar•io

scenary : **scen•ery**
sceneario : **sce•nar•io**
scen•ery
sceptacism : **skep•ti•cism**
scep•ter
scep•tic; **skep•tic**
scepticism : **skep•ti•cism**
sceptor : **scep•ter**
scetch : **sketch**
sched•ule
scheme
schism
schitzophrenia :
    schizo•phre•nia
schizephrenia :
    schizo•phre•nia
schizm : **schism**
schizo•phre•nia
scho•lar
scholer : **scho•lar**
schollar : **scho•lar**
sciance : **sci•ence**
sci•ence
scisors : **scis•sors**
scissers : **scis•sors**
scis•sors
scithe : **scythe**
scorpian : **scor•pi•on**
scorpien : **scor•pi•on**
scor•pi•on
scour
scrach : **scratch**
scratch
scrimage : **scrim•mage**

scrim•mage
scrimmege : **scrim•mage**
scrimmige : **scrim•mage**
scrutenize : **scru•ti•nize**
scru•ti•nize
sculpter : **sculp•tor**
sculp•tor
sculp•ture
scythe
seasen : **sea•son**
seasin : **sea•son**
sea•son
secand : **sec•ond**
se•cede
seceed : **se•cede**
secind : **sec•ond**
sec•ond
secracy : **se•cre•cy**
secratary : **sec•re•tary**
se•cre•cy
secresy : **se•cre•cy**
sec•re•tary
secretery : **sec•re•tary**
secritary : **sec•re•tary**
sec•u•lar
seculer : **sec•u•lar**
securaty : **se•cu•ri•ty**
se•cu•ri•ty
securrity : **se•cu•ri•ty**
sedament : **sed•i•ment**
sedar : **ce•dar** (tree);
    se•der (Passover)
sed•a•tive

se•der (Passover); ce•dar (tree)

sed•i•ment

seditive : sed•a•tive

segragate : seg•re•gate

seg•re•gate

segrigate : seg•re•gate

seige : siege

seive : sieve

seis•mic

seldem : sel•dom

sel•dom

selestial : ce•les•tial

seman : se•men

se•men

sem•i•nar

senater : sen•a•tor

sen•a•tor

sence : sense

senier : se•nior

se•nile

se•nior

sensable : sen•si•ble

sense

senser : cen•ser (incense); cen•sor (examine and remove); sen•sor (senses)

sensery : sen•so•ry

sen•si•ble

sen•sor (senses); cen•ser (incense); cen•sor (examine and remove)

sen•so•ry

sen•su•al

sensuel : sen•su•al

sensus : cen•sus

sentament : sen•ti•ment

sen•ti•ment

sentimeter : cen•ti•me•ter

sep•a•rate

seperate : sep•a•rate

septer : scep•ter

sequance : se•quence

se•quence

sequense : se•quence

sequince : se•quence

seremony : cer•e•mo•ny

se•rene

ser•geant

sergent : ser•geant

sergeon : sur•geon

serine : se•rene

se•ri•ous

sermen : ser•mon

ser•mon

serpant : ser•pent

ser•pent

ser•vant

servent : ser•vant

servicable : ser•vice•a•ble

ser•vice•a•ble

ses•a•me

sesede : se•cede

sesime : ses•a•me

sessame : ses•a•me

sessimy : ses•a•me

seveer : se•vere

se•vere
sex•u•al
sexuel : **sex•u•al**
shadoe : **shad•ow**
shad•ow
shakey : **shak•y**
shak•y
shampagne : **cham•pagne**
shampaign : **cham•pagne**
shandelier : **chan•de•lier**
shauffeur : **chauf•feur**
sheild : **shield**
shepard : **shep•herd**
shephard : **shep•herd**
shep•herd
shepperd : **shep•herd**
sherbert : **sher•bet**
sher•bet
sher•iff
sherriff : **sher•iff**
shield
shiffon : **chif•fon**
shivalry : **chiv•al•ry**
sholder : **shoul•der**
shoul•der
shovelled : **shov•eled**
shovinist : **chau•vin•ist**
shreik : **shriek**
shrewd
shriek
sianide : **cy•a•nide**
sianyde : **cy•a•nide**
sibernetics :
  cy•ber•net•ics

siberpunk : **cy•ber•punk**
sicamore : **syc•a•more**
sicle : **cy•cle**
siclone : **cy•clone**
siege
siesmic : **seis•mic**
sieve
sifer : **ci•fer**
sig•na•ture
signiture : **sig•na•ture**
silance : **si•lence**
si•lence
silense : **si•lence**
sil•hou•ette
sillable : **syl•la•ble**
silouette : **sil•hou•ette**
simbal : **cym•bal**
  (instrument); **sym•bol**
  (sign)
sinanym : **syn•o•nym**
sin•cere
sincereity : **sin•cer•i•ty**
sin•cer•i•ty
sinder : **cin•der**
sinema : **cin•e•ma**
sing•u•lar
singuler : **sing•u•lar**
sinical : **cyn•i•cal**
sinsere : **sin•cere**
sinthesize : **syn•the•size**
sir•up : syr•up
sitadel : **cit•a•del**
sitizen : **cit•i•zen**
sizemic : **seis•mic**

skald : **scald**
skech : **sketch**
skelaten : **skel•e•ton**
skelaton : **skel•e•ton**
skel•e•ton
skeptacism : **skep•ti•cism**
skep•tic : scep•tic
skep•ti•cism
skeptisism : **skep•ti•cism**
sketch
skied
skiied : **skied**
ski•ing
skiis : **skis**
skis
skour : **scour**
slaigh : **sleigh** (sled); **slay** (kill)
slaugh•ter
slauter : **slaugh•ter**
slavary : **slav•ery**
slav•ery
slay (kill); **sleigh** (sled)
sleasy : **slea•zy**
slea•zy
sleezy : **slea•zy**
sleigh (sled); **slay** (kill)
sleuth
slewth : **sleuth**
sliegh : **sleigh** (sled); **slay** (kill)
slimey : **sli•my**
sli•my
slipery : **slip•per•y**

slip•per•y
slo•gan
slogen : **slo•gan**
smokey : **smok•y**
smok•y
smudge
smuge : **smudge**
snob•ber•y
snobery : **snob•ber•y**
soberiety : **so•bri•e•ty**
so•bri•e•ty
so•cia•ble
sociaty : **so•ci•e•ty**
so•ci•e•ty
sodder : **sol•der**
soffen : **soft•en**
sofisticated : **so•phis•ti•cat•ed**
sofomore : **soph•o•more**
sof•ten
so•lace
so•lar
solataire : **sol•i•taire**
sol•der
sole•ly
solem : **sol•emn**
sol•emn
soler : **so•lar**
solice : **so•lace**
so•lic•it
sol•id
solilaquy : **so•lil•o•quy**
soliliquy : **so•lil•o•quy**
so•lil•oquy

solisit : **so•lic•it**
sol•i•taire
solled : **sol•id**
sollid : **sol•id**
soluable : **sol•u•ble**
sol•u•ble
soluible : **sol•u•ble**
solveable : **solv•a•ble**
solv•a•ble
soly : **sole•ly**
som•er•sault :
   sum•mer•sault
sommersault :
   som•er•sault :
   sum•mer•sault
so•na•ta
sonatta : **so•na•ta**
sonet : **son•net**
son•net
sophistacated :
   so•phis•ti•cat•ed
so•phis•ti•cat•ed
sophmore : **soph•o•more**
soph•o•more
sor•cer•er
sorceror : **sor•cer•er**
so•ror•i•ty
sororrity : **so•ror•i•ty**
souvanir : **sou•ve•nir**
sou•ve•nir
sov•er•eign
soverin : **sov•er•eign**
spacial : **spa•tial**
spa•cious

spagetti : **spa•ghet•ti**
spagheti : **spa•ghet•ti**
spa•ghet•ti
sparcity : **spar•si•ty**
spar•si•ty
spasm
spat•ial
spatious : **spa•cious**
spat•u•la
spazm : **spasm**
spear (weapon); **sphere**
   (ball)
spe•cial
speciel : **spe•cial**
speciman : **spec•i•men**
spec•i•men
spec•ta•cle
specticle : **spec•ta•cle**
spedometer :
   speed•om•e•ter
speed•om•e•ter
spere : **spear** (weapon);
   sphere (ball)
sphere (ball); **spear**
   (weapon)
sphinx
spin•ach
spinich : **spin•ach**
spiret : **spir•it**
spir•it
spir•i•tu•al
spirituel : **spir•i•tu•al**
splender : **splen•dor**
splen•dor

sponser : **spon•sor**
spon•sor
spontanaity :
   spon•ta•ne•i•ty
spontenaity :
   spon•ta•ne•i•ty
spon•ta•ne•i•ty
spon•ta•ne•ous
spontanious :
   spon•ta•ne•ous
squal•id
squallid : **squal•id**
squauk : **squawk**
squawk
squeal
squea•mish
sqeemish : **squea•mish**
squimish : **squea•mish**
squirel : **squir•rel**
squirl : **squir•rel**
squir•rel
sqwauk : **squawk**
stacato : **stac•ca•to**
stac•ca•to
staccatto : **stac•ca•to**
stadiem : **sta•di•um**
sta•di•um
stair (step); stare (look)
stalion : **stal•lion**
stallian : **stal•lion**
stal•lion
stampead : **stam•pede**
stam•pede
stan•dard

standerd : **stan•dard**
stapel : **sta•ple**
sta•ple
stare (look); **stair** (step)
stareotype : **ste•reo•type**
starile : **ster•ile**
sta•tion•ary (not
   moving); **sta•tion•ery**
   (paper)
sta•tion•ery (paper);
   sta•tion•ary
   (not moving)
stat•ue
stea•dy
stel•lar
steller : **stel•lar**
stencell : **sten•cil**
sten•cil
stensil : **sten•cil**
steralize : **ster•il•ize**
ste•re•o•type
ster•ile
sterilise (British) :
   ster•il•ize
ster•il•ize
steriotype : **ste•re•o•type**
stich : **stitch**
stiffle : **sti•fle**
sti•fle
sti•let•to
stilleto : **sti•let•to**
stimulous : **stim•u•lus**
stim•u•lus
stirrip : **stir•rup**

stir•rup
stirup : **stir•rup**
stitch
stom•ach
stomache : **stom•ach**
stomack : **stom•ach**
stor•age
storeage : **stor•age**
storidge : **stor•age**
straight (not bent); **strait**
  (water; distress)
strait (water; distress);
  straight (not bent)
stratagy : **strat•e•gy**
strate : **straight**
  (not bent); **strait** (water;
  distress)
strat•e•gy
stratigy : **strat•e•gy**
strech : **stretch**
strength
stretch
stubbern : **stub•born**
stub•born
stuborn : **stub•born**
stuc•co
stucko : **stuc•co**
stuco : **stuc•co**
stu•dio
suade : **suede**
subbordinate :
  sub•or•di•nate
subordinent :
  sub•or•di•nate

sub•or•di•nate
subpeona : **sub•poe•na**
subpina : **sub•poe•na**
sub•poe•na
subsequant : **sub•se•quent**
sub•se•quent
subserviant :
  sub•ser•vi•ent
sub•ser•vi•ent
subsidary : **sub•sid•i•ar•y**
sub•sid•i•ar•y
sub•si•dy
subsiquent : **sub•se•quent**
sub•sti•tute
subtel : **sub•tle**
sub•tle
sub•urb
suc•ceed
suceed : **suc•ceed**
suede
sufficate : **suf•fo•cate**
suf•fo•cate
sug•ar
suger : **sug•ar**
suggestable :
  sug•gest•i•ble
sug•gest•i•ble
su•i•cide
suiside : **su•i•cide**
suit•a•ble
suitible : **suit•a•ble**
sumary : **sum•ma•ry**
sum•ma•ry

sum•mer•sault :
   som•er•sault
summery : **sum•ma•ry**
superier : **su•pe•ri•or**
superintendant :
   su•per•in•ten•dent
su•per•in•ten•dent
su•pe•ri•or
supertendent :
   su•per•in•ten•dent
suppina : **sub•poe•na**
sup•ple•ment
suppliment :
   sup•ple•ment
suprise : **sur•prise**
surgean : **sur•geon**
sur•geon
surgion : **sur•geon**
surogate : **sur•ro•gate**
sur•prise
surprize : **sur•prise**
sur•ro•gate
survaillance :
   sur•veil•lance
sur•veil•lance
surveillence :
   sur•veil•lance
surveyer : **sur•vey•or**
sur•vey•or
suspence : **sus•pense**
sus•pense
sus•pi•cion
suspision : **sus•pi•cion**
sustainance : **sus•te•nance**

sus•te•nance
sustenence : **sus•te•nance**
sutle : **sub•tle**
swastica : **swas•ti•ka**
swas•ti•ka
swival : **swiv•el**
swiv•el
sybernetics :
   cy•ber•net•ics
syberpunk : **cy•ber•punk**
syc•a•more
syclone : **cy•clone**
sylable : **syl•la•ble**
sylabus : **syl•la•bus**
syl•la•ble
syl•la•bus
syllible : **syl•la•ble**
sym•bol (sign); **cym•bal**
   (instrument)
synical : **cyn•i•cal**
symetry : **sym•me•try**
symmatry : **sym•me•try**
sym•me•try
symptem : **symp•tom**
symp•tom
synecal : **cyn•i•cal**
synonim : **syn•o•nym**
syn•o•nym
synthasize : **syn•the•size**
syn•the•size
syr•up
systam : **sys•tem**
sys•tem
systum : **sys•tem**

Tt

tabbernacle :
 tab•er•na•cle
tabblet : **tab•let**
tabblou : **tab•leau**
tabboo : **ta•boo**
tabernacal : **tab•er•na•cle**
tab•er•na•cle
tab•leau
tab•let
tablett : **tab•let**
ta•boo
tacet : **tac•it**
tac•it
tacitern : **tac•i•turn**
tac•i•turn
tact•ful
tactfull : **tact•ful**
tafeta : **taf•fe•ta**
taf•fe•ta
taffetta : **taf•fe•ta**
taffita : **taf•fe•ta**
tailer : **tai•lor**
tailight : **tail•light**
tail•light
tai•lor
take•o•ver

takover : **take•o•ver**
talant : **tal•ent**
talcem : **tal•cum**
tal•cum
talelight : **tail•light**
talen : **tal•on**
tal•ent
talk•a•tive
talkitive : **talk•a•tive**
tallent : **tal•ent**
tallon : **tal•on**
tal•on
tamborine : **tam•bou•rine**
tam•bou•rine
tangeble : **tan•gi•ble**
tan•gi•ble
tan•ta•lize
tantellize : **tan•ta•lize**
tantilize : **tan•ta•lize**
tapeoca : **tap•i•o•ca**
tap•i•o•ca
tappioca : **tap•i•o•ca**
taranchulla : **ta•ran•tu•la**
ta•ran•tu•la
tar•iff
tarpalin : **tar•pau•lin**

tar•pau•lin
tarpellin : **tar•pau•lin**
tarpolin : **tar•pau•lin**
tarrantula : **ta•ran•tu•la**
tarrif : **tar•iff**
tarriff : **tar•iff**
tas•sel
tassiturn : **tac•i•turn**
tassle : **tas•sel**
tatoo : **tat•too**
tat•too
taught (teach); **taut**
  (tight); **tot** (child)
taut (tight); **taught**
  (teach); **tot** (child)
taylor : **tai•lor**
tea (drink); **tee** (golf)
teadious : **te•dious**
team (group); **teem**
  (swarm)
tease
teaze : **tease**
tech•ni•cal
techniche : **tech•nique**
technicle : **tech•ni•cal**
tech•nique
tecnical : **tech•ni•cal**
tecnichal : **tech•ni•cal**
tecnique : **tech•nique**
tedeous : **te•dious**
te•di•ous
tedius : **te•di•ous**
tee (golf); **tea** (drink)

teem (swarm); **team**
  (group)
teeth (noun); **teethe** (verb)
teethe (verb); **teeth** (noun)
teeze : **tease**
telagram : **tel•e•gram**
telaphone : **tel•e•phone**
telascope : **tel•e•scope**
telavision : **tel•e•vi•sion**
tel•e•gram
tel•e•phone
tel•e•scope
tel•e•vi•sion
teligram : **tel•e•gram**
teliphone : **tel•e•phone**
teliscope : **tel•e•scope**
telivision : **tel•e•vi•sion**
tellaphone : **tel•e•phone**
tellivision : **tel•e•vi•sion**
telltail : **tell•tale**
tell•tale
teltale : **tell•tale**
temparary : **tem•po•rar•y**
tem•per•ance
temperary : **tem•po•rar•y**
tem•per•a•ture
temperence :
  tem•per•ance
temperture :
  tem•per•a•ture
tem•po•rary
temprature :
  tem•per•a•ture
tenacle : **ten•ta•cle**

tenament : **ten•e•ment**
ten•ant
tenden : **ten•don**
tendin : **ten•don**
ten•don
ten•e•ment
tenent : **ten•ant**
tener : **ten•or**
tenis : **ten•nis**
ten•nis
tennuous : **ten•u•ous**
ten•or
ten•sion
ten•ta•cle
tenticle : **ten•ta•cle**
tention : **ten•sion**
ten•u•ous
terace : **ter•race**
terain : **ter•rain**
teradactyl : **pter•o•dac•tyl**
terantula : **ta•ran•tu•la**
terban : **tur•ban**
terific : **ter•ri•fic**
teritory : **ter•ri•to•ry**
ter•mi•nal
terminel : **ter•mi•nal**
terodactyl : **pter•o•dac•tyl**
terquoise : **tur•quoise**
ter•race
ter•rain
terraine : **ter•rain**
terrane : **ter•rain**
terrany : **tyr•an•ny**
terrece : **ter•race**

terrice : **ter•race**
terriffic : **ter•ri•fic**
ter•ri•fic
ter•ri•to•ry
testafy : **tes•ti•fy**
tes•ti•fy
Teusday : **Tues•day**
thach : **thatch**
thatch
theary : **the•o•ry**
the•a•ter : **the•a•tre**
the•a•tre : **the•a•ter**
theif : **thief**
their (possessive); **there** (place); **they•re** (contraction)
theivery : **thiev•er•y**
the•o•rem
theorum : **the•o•rem**
the•o•ry
ther•a•peu•tic
theraputic : **ther•a•peu•tic**
ther•a•py
there (place); **their** (possessive); **they•re** (contraction)
therepy : **ther•a•py**
thermas : **ther•mos**
ther•mos
thermus : **ther•mos**
thesauras : **the•saur•us**
the•sau•rus
thesorus : **the•sau•rus**
they're (contraction);

their (possessive);
there (place)
thief
thievary : **thiev•er•y**
thiev•ery
thigh
thir•ti•eth
thirtyeth : **thir•ti•eth**
thisle : **this•tle**
thissel : **this•tle**
this•tle
thorogh : **thor•ough**
   (complete); **through**
   (preposition)
thor•ough (complete);
   through (preposition)
thourough : **thor•ough**
   (complete); **through**
   (preposition)
thou•sand
thousend : **thou•sand**
thread
thred : **thread**
threshhold : **thresh•old**
thresh•old
through (preposition);
   thor•ough (complete)
thumb
thum : **thumb**
ti•ger
tigger : **ti•ger**
tight
tim•ber (wood); **tim•bre**
   (sound)

tim•bre (sound); **tim•ber**
   (wood)
tin•sel
tinsell : **tin•sel**
tinsil : **tin•sel**
tinsle : **tin•sel**
tipewriter : **type•writ•er**
tiphoon : **ty•phoon**
tipical : **typ•i•cal**
tiranny : **tyr•an•ny**
tissoue : **tis•sue**
tis•sue
titilate : **tit•il•late**
tit•il•late
tittillate : **tit•il•late**
toast
to•bac•co
tobaco : **to•bac•co**
tobbacco : **to•bac•co**
tobboggan : **to•bog•gan**
tobbogin : **to•bog•gan**
to•bog•gan
toboggen : **to•bog•gan**
tobogon : **to•bo•g•gan**
tofee : **tof•fee**
tof•fee
toi•let
toilit : **toi•let**
to•ken
tokin : **to•ken**
tol•er•ance
tolerence : **tol•er•ance**
tollerance : **tol•er•ance**
to•ma•to

tomatoe : **to•ma•to**
to•ma•toes
tomatos : **to•ma•toes**
tomb•stone
tommorow : **to•mor•row**
tommorrow : **to•mor•row**
tomorow : **to•mor•row**
to•mor•row
tonge : **tongue**
tongue
to•night
tonite : **to•night**
tonsel : **ton•sil**
ton•sil
tonsill : **ton•sil**
top•ic
topick : **top•ic**
toppic : **top•ic**
tor•na•do
tornato : **tor•na•do**
tor•pe•do
torpido : **tor•pe•do**
torrpeto : **tor•pe•do**
tor•sion
tortice : **tor•toise**
tortila : **tor•ti•lla**
tor•ti•lla
tortion : **tor•sion**
tortise : **tor•toise**
tortiya : **tor•ti•lla**
tor•toise
tor•tu•ous
tor•ture
torturous : **tor•tu•ous**

toste : **toast**
tot (child); **taught** (teach);
    taut (tight)
to•tal
totall : **to•tal**
totam : **to•tem**
totel : **to•tal**
to•tem
totum : **to•tem**
tough
toulip : **tu•lip**
toumbstone : **tomb•stone**
toumstone : **tomb•stone**
tounge : **tongue**
tou•pee
tour•na•ment
tourniment :
    tour•na•ment
tow•el
towl : **tow•el**
trac•ta•ble
tracter : **trac•tor**
tractible : **trac•ta•ble**
trac•tor
tradegy : **trag•e•dy**
tradgedy : **trag•e•dy**
traf•fic
traffick : **traf•fic**
trafic : **traf•fic**
trag•e•dy
tragidy : **trag•e•dy**
trail
traiter : **trai•tor**
trai•tor

trajectery : **tra•jec•to•ry**
tra•jec•to•ry
trale : **trail**
trama : **trau•ma**
trampaline : **tram•po•line**
trampalene : **tram•po•line**
tram•po•line
trancend : **tran•scend**
trancsend : **tran•scend**
tran•quil
tranquill : **tran•quil**
tran•scend
transend : **tran•scend**
transexual :
   trans•sex•u•al
trans•sex•u•al
transferance :
   trans•fer•ence
trans•fer•ence
transferrence :
   trans•fer•ence
transiant : **tran•sient**
tran•sient
trapazoid : **trap•e•zoid**
trapeeze : **tra•peze**
trapese : **tra•peze**
tra•peze
trap•e•zoid
trapezoyd : **trap•e•zoid**
trapizoid : **trap•e•zoid**
trasen : **trea•son**
trau•ma
trav•el
travil : **trav•el**

travvel : **trav•el**
treachary : **treach•er•y**
treach•er•y
trea•son
trea•sure
treatase : **trea•tise**
treatice : **trea•tise**
trea•tise
trebal : **tre•ble**
trebble : **tre•ble**
tre•ble
trechery : **treach•ery**
tremer : **trem•or**
trem•or
treson : **trea•son**
tres•pass
tresspass : **tres•pass**
tresure : **trea•sure**
trib•al
tribel : **trib•al**
trilegy : **tril•o•gy**
triligy : **tril•o•gy**
tril•o•gy
trin•ket
trinkit : **trin•ket**
tri•ple
tripple : **tri•ple**
triumff : **tri•umph**
tri•umph
trivea : **triv•ia**
triv•ia
trol•ley
trolly : **trol•ley**
trop•i•cal

tropicle : **trop•i•cal**
trou•sers
trouzers : **trou•sers**
trow•el
trowl : **trow•el**
tru•ant
truely : **tru•ly**
truent : **tru•ant**
tru•ly
tsar : **czar**
tuelip : **tu•lip**
Tues•day
tuff : **tough**
tu•lip
tulipp : **tu•lip**
tumer : **tu•mor**
tumestone : **tomb•stone**
tu•mor
tunell : **tun•nel**
tungue : **tongue**
tun•nel
tunnle : **tun•nel**
tupee : **tou•pee**
tur•ban
turben : **tur•ban**
turbin : **tur•ban**

tur•key
turky : **tur•key**
turnament : **tour•na•ment**
tur•quoise
tur•ret
turrit : **tur•ret**
Tusday : **Tues•day**
Tuseday : **Tues•day**
tuter : **tu•tor**
tu•tor
tux•e•do
tuxido : **tux•e•do**
tweesers : **twee•zers**
twee•zers
twelfth
twelth : **twelfth**
twelvth : **twelfth**
type•writ•er
ty•phoon
typ•i•cal
typicle : **typ•i•cal**
tyr•an•ny
tyrany : **tyr•an•ny**
tyrranny : **tyr•an•ny**
tyrrany : **tyr•an•ny**
tzar : **tsar ; czar**

Uu

ubiquatice : **u•biq•ui•tous**
u•biq•ui•tous
ubiquitus : **u•biq•ui•tous**
Ucharist : **Eu•cha•rist**
ud•der (cow); **ut•ter**
  (total)
ufamism : **eu•phe•mism**
ug•li•ness
uglyness : **ug•li•ness**
ukalale : **u•ku•le•le**
ukelele : **u•ku•le•le**
ukileley : **u•ku•le•le**
u•ku•le•le
ul•cer
ulogy : **eu•lo•gy**
ulser : **ul•cer**
ulteirior : **ul•te•ri•or**
ulterier : **ul•te•ri•or**
ul•te•ri•or
ulterviolet : **ul•tra•vi•o•let**
ul•ti•mate
ultimite : **ul•ti•mate**
ul•tra•vi•o•let
umbilacal : **um•bil•i•cal**
um•bil•i•cal
umbillical : **um•bil•i•cal**

umbrela : **um•brel•la**
um•brel•la
umpier : **um•pire**
umpior : **um•pire**
um•pire
unabel : **un•ab•le**
un•ab•le
un•a•bridged
unabriged : **un•a•bridged**
un•ac•count•able
unaccountible :
  un•ac•count•able
unacorn : **u•ni•corn**
unacountable :
  un•ac•count•able
unafy : **u•ni•fy**
unanamous :
  u•nan•i•mous
u•nan•i•mous
unanimus : **u•nan•i•mous**
unason : **u•ni•son**
unatural : **un•nat•u•ral**
unaverse : **u•ni•verse**
unaversity : **u•ni•ver•si•ty**
unbeleivable :
  un•be•liev•a•ble

un•be•liev•a•ble
unbelieveable :
  un•be•liev•a•ble
unbelievible :
  un•be•liev•a•ble
unbudgeing :
  un•budg•ing
un•budg•ing
unbuging : **un•budg•ing**
uncal : **un•cle**
unceramonious :
  un•cer•e•mon•i•ous
un•cer•e•mon•i•ous
uncerimonius :
  un•cer•e•mon•i•ous
un•cle
un•con•di•tion•al
unc•tu•ous
un•de•ni•a•ble
undenyable :
  un•de•ni•a•ble
un•der•grad•u•ate
undergraduite :
  un•der•grad•u•ate
un•der•neath
undertoe : **un•der•tow**
un•der•tow
underwair : **un•der•wear**
underware : **un•der•wear**
un•der•wear
unequivacle :
  un•e•quiv•o•cal
unequivical :
  un•e•quiv•o•cal

un•e•quiv•o•cal
unferl : **un•furl**
un•furl
unholesome :
  un•whole•some
uniche : **u•nique**
un•i•corn
u•ni•fy
u•nique
u•ni•son
u•nit (noun); **u•nite** (verb)
u•nite (verb); **u•nit** (noun)
univercity : **u•ni•ver•si•ty**
u•ni•ver•sal
universaty : **u•ni•ver•si•ty**
u•ni•verse
universel : **u•ni•ver•sal**
u•ni•ver•si•ty
unkle : **un•cle**
un•liv•a•ble
unliveable : **un•liv•a•ble**
un•nat•u•ral
unnatureal : **un•nat•u•ral**
unnify : **u•ni•fy**
un•pal•at•able
unpalateable :
  un•pal•at•able
unpalatible :
  un•pal•at•able
unpaletable :
  un•pal•at•able
unpallatable :
  un•pal•at•able

unprecadented :
   un•prec•e•dent•ed
un•prec•e•dent•ed
unprecidented :
   un•prec•e•dent•ed
unpresedented :
   un•prec•e•dent•ed
un•rav•el
unravle : **un•rav•el**
un•re•li•a•ble
unrelyable : **un•re•li•a•ble**
unrelyible : **un•re•li•a•ble**
un•ri•valed : un•ri•valled
un•ri•valled : un•ri•valed
unriveled : **un•ri•valed :**
   un•ri•valled
unrivelled : **un•ri•valed :**
   un•ri•valled
unruley : **un•ru•ly**
un•ru•ly
unsanatary :
   un•san•i•tar•y
un•san•i•tar•y
unsanitery :
   un•san•i•tar•y
unsavery : **un•sa•vor•y**
un•sa•vor•y
un•scathed
un•speak•a•ble
unspeakible :
   un•speak•a•ble
untel : **un•til**
un•til
untill : **un•til**

un•time•ly
untimly : **un•time•ly**
unuch : **eu•nuch**
un•u•su•al
unusuel : **un•u•su•al**
unvail : **un•veil**
unvale : **un•veil**
un•veil
unweildy : **un•wield•y**
un•whole•some
unwhollsome :
   un•whole•some
unwholsome :
   un•whole•some
un•wieldy
upbrade : **up•braid**
up•braid
up•heav•al
upheaveal : **up•heav•al**
upheavel : **up•heav•al**
uphemism : **eu•phe•mism**
upholestery :
   up•hol•ster•y
upholstary : **up•hol•ster•y**
up•hol•ster•y
upholstory : **up•hol•ster•y**
upholstry : **up•hol•ster•y**
uphoria : **eu•pho•ri•a**
u•pon
uproareous :
   up•roar•i•ous
up•roar•i•ous
uproarius : **up•roar•i•ous**
uprorious : **up•roar•i•ous**

upwholstery :
  up•hol•stery
uraniam : **u•ra•ni•um**
u•ra•ni•um
ur•ban (city); **ur•bane**
  (polished)
ur•bane (polished);
  ur•ban (city)
urchan : **ur•chin**
urchen : **ur•chin**
ur•chin
urin : **ur•ine**
ur•i•nal
ur•ine
urinel : **ur•i•nal**
urn
us•a•ble
us•age
useable : **us•a•ble**
use•ful
usefull : **use•ful**
usege : **us•age**
useing : **us•ing**
userp : **u•surp**
usible : **us•a•ble**
usige : **us•age**
us•ing
usu•al•ly
usualy : **us•u•al•ly**
usully : **us•u•al•ly**

u•surp
utalize : **u•ti•lize**
utelize : **u•ti•lize**
utencil : **u•ten•sil**
utensal : **u•ten•sil**
utensel : **u•ten•sil**
u•ten•sil
utensill : **u•ten•sil**
uteras : **u•ter•us**
uteris : **u•ter•us**
u•ter•us
uthanasia : **eu•tha•na•sia**
uthinasia : **eu•tha•na•sia**
utilatarien :
  u•til•i•tar•i•an
utilaty : **u•til•i•ty**
utilety : **u•til•i•ty**
u•til•i•tar•i•an
u•til•i•ty
u•ti•lize
utillitarian :
  u•til•i•tar•i•an
utillity : **u•til•i•ty**
utopea : **u•to•pia**
u•to•pia
ut•ter (total; express);
  ud•der (cow)
ut•ter•ance
utterence : **ut•ter•ance**
uturus : **u•ter•us**

Vv

vacacian : **va•ca•tion**
va•can•cy
vacansy : **va•can•cy**
va•cant
vacasion : **va•ca•tion**
vacatian : **va•ca•tion**
va•ca•tion
vaccant : **va•cant**
vac•cine
vaccum : **vac•u•um**
vacellate : **vac•il•late**
vacency : **va•can•cy**
vacene : **vac•cine**
vacent : **va•cant**
vacilate : **vac•il•late**
va•cil•late
vacine : **vac•cine**
vacinity : **vi•cin•i•ty**
vacsine : **vac•cine**
vacume : **vac•u•um**
vac•u•ous
vac•u•um
vag•a•bond
vacuus : **vac•u•ous**
va•grant
vagrent : **va•grant**

vagrint : **va•grant**
vain (conceited); **vane**
  (weather); **vein** (blood)
vaiporize : **va•por•ize**
valay : **val•et**
valadictorian :
  val•e•dic•to•ri•an
valantine : **val•en•tine**
valed : **val•id**
val•e•dic•to•ri•an
val•en•tine
valer : **val•or**
valese : **va•lise**
val•et
valey : **val•ley**
val•i•ant
val•id
validictorian :
  val•e•dic•to•ri•an
valient : **val•iant**
valintine : **val•en•tine**
va•lise
valize : **va•lise**
vallentine : **val•en•tine**
vallet : **va•let**
val•ley

vallid : **val•id**
vallor : **val•or**
valluable : **val•u•a•ble**
vally : **val•ley**
val•or
val•u•a•ble
valuble : **val•u•a•ble**
valueable : **val•u•a•ble**
vampier : **vam•pire**
vam•pire
van•dal
vandel : **van•dal**
vandetta : **ven•det•ta**
vane (weather); **vain**
  (conceited); **vein**
  (blood)
vanety : **van•i•ty**
vanila : **va•nil•la**
va•nil•la
van•i•ty
vannilla : **va•nil•la**
vaperize : **va•por•ize**
va•por•ize
varanda : **ve•ran•da**
varcity : **var•si•ty**
var•i•a•ble
var•i•a•tion
variaty : **va•ri•e•ty**
var•i•cose
va•ri•ety
var•i•ous
varius : **var•i•ous**
varsaty : **var•si•ty**
varsety : **var•si•ty**

var•si•ty
varyable : **var•i•a•ble**
vasillate : **vac•il•late**
vaude•ville
vaudville : **vaude•ville**
vaxine : **vac•cine**
vegabond : **vag•a•bond**
veg•e•ta•ble
vegetible : **veg•e•ta•ble**
vegitable : **veg•e•ta•ble**
vegtable : **veg•e•ta•ble**
vehamence : **ve•he•mence**
vehemance : **ve•he•mence**
ve•he•mence
vehemense : **ve•he•mence**
vehical : **ve•hi•cle**
ve•hi•cle
veicle : **ve•hi•cle**
vein (blood); **vain**
  (conceited); **vane**
  (weather)
veiw : **view**
vellocity : **ve•loc•i•ty**
ve•loc•i•ty
velosity : **ve•loc•i•ty**
vel•vet
velvit : **vel•vet**
venam : **ven•om**
venareal : **ve•ne•re•al**
venason : **ven•i•son**
vend•er ; vend•or
ven•det•ta
vend•or ; vend•er
ve•neer

veneir : **ve•neer**

venem : **ven•om**

ve•ne•re•al

venerial : **ve•ne•re•al**

vengance : **ven•geance**

ven•geance

vengence : **ven•geance**

venim : **ven•om**

ven•i•son

ven•om

ven•ti•late

ventillate : **ven•ti•late**

ventrilaquist :
  ven•tril•o•quist

ventrilloquist :
  ven•tril•o•quist

ven•tril•o•quist

ve•ran•da

verbatem : **ver•ba•tim**

ver•ba•tim

verbatum : **ver•ba•tim**

verces : **ver•sus**

ver•dict

vergin : **vir•gin**

vericose : **var•i•cose**

ver•i•fy

verile : **vir•ile**

verilly : **ver•i•ly**

ver•i•ly

vermilian : **ver•mil•ion**

ver•mil•ion

vermillion : **ver•mil•ion**

vermooth : **ver•mouth**

ver•mouth

ver•nac•u•lar

vernaculer : **ver•nac•u•lar**

verranda : **ve•ran•da**

verrify : **ver•i•fy**

ver•sa•tile

versatill : **ver•sa•tile**

versetile : **ver•sa•tile**

versis : **ver•sus**

versitile : **ver•sa•tile**

ver•sus

vertabrae : **ver•te•brae**

vertago : **ver•ti•go**

ver•te•brae

vertebray : **ver•te•brae**

vertibrae : **ver•te•brae**

ver•ti•cal

verticle : **ver•ti•cal**

ver•ti•go

vertue : **vir•tue**

ver•y

vessal : **ves•sel**

ves•sel

vessle : **ves•sel**

vestabule : **ves•ti•bule**

vestage : **ves•tige**

vestege : **ves•tige**

ves•ti•bule

ves•tige

vet•er•an

veteranarian :
  vet•er•i•nar•i•an

veteren : **vet•er•an**

veterenarian :
  vet•er•i•nar•i•an

veterin : **vet•er•an**
vet•er•i•nar•i•an
ve•to
vetoe : **ve•to**
ve•toes
vetos : **ve•toes**
vetranarian :
  vet•er•i•nar•i•an
vetrinarian :
  vet•er•i•nar•i•an
viabal : **vi•a•ble**
vi•a•ble
vial (bottle); **vile** (base)
vialate : **vi•o•late**
vialin : **vi•o•lin**
viallin : **vi•o•lin**
vi•bra•tor
vibrater : **vi•bra•tor**
vic•ar
vicareous : **vi•car•i•ous**
vi•car•i•ous
vicer : **vic•ar**
vicinaty : **vi•cin•i•ty**
vi•cin•i•ty
vi•cious
vicisitude : **vi•cis•si•tude**
vi•cis•si•tude
victary : **vic•to•ry**
victem : **vic•tim**
victery : **vic•to•ry**
vic•tim
vic•to•ry
vid•eo
vidio : **vid•eo**

view
vigelant : **vig•i•lant**
viger : **vig•or**
vig•i•lant
vigilent : **vig•i•lant**
vigillant : **vig•i•lant**
vignet : **vi•gnette**
vi•gnette
vig•or
vilage : **vil•lage**
vilain : **vil•lain**
vilate : **vi•o•late**
vile (base); **vial** (bottle)
vilan : **vil•lain**
vilin : **vil•lain**
vil•lage
vil•lain
villate : **vi•o•late**
villege : **vil•lage**
villen : **vil•lain**
villidge : **vil•lage**
villige : **vil•lage**
villin : **vil•lain**
vinager : **vin•e•gar**
vin•e•gar
vineger : **vin•e•gar**
vinel : **vi•nyl**
vine•yard
vinigar : **vin•e•gar**
vinil : **vi•nyl**
vinill : **vi•nyl**
vin•tage
vintege : **vin•tage**
vintige : **vin•tage**

vinyard : **vine•yard**
vinyette : **vi•gnette**
vi•nyl
vi•o•late
vi•o•lin
vi•per
vipor : **vi•per**
viras : **vi•rus**
virgen : **vir•gin**
vir•gin
vir•ile
viris : **vi•rus**
vir•tue
virtueous : **vir•tu•ous**
virtuis : **vir•tu•ous**
vir•tu•ous
vi•rus
visability : **vis•i•bil•i•ty**
visater : **vis•i•tor**
viscious : **vi•cious**
vis•cous
viser : **vi•sor**
visibilaty : **vis•i•bil•i•ty**
vis•i•bil•i•ty
visibillity : **vis•i•bil•i•ty**
visinity : **vi•cin•i•ty**
visiter : **vis•i•tor**
vis•i•tor
vi•sor
vississitude :
    vi•cis•si•tude
vis•u•al
visuel : **vis•u•al**
vi•tal

vitamen : **vi•ta•min**
vi•ta•min
vitel : **vi•tal**
vitimin : **vi•ta•min**
vivacaty : **vi•vac•i•ty**
vi•vac•i•ty
vivasity : **vi•vac•i•ty**
vixan : **vix•en**
vix•en
vixin : **vix•en**
vizer : **vi•sor**
vo•cab•u•lary
vocabulery :
    vo•cab•u•lary
vo•cal
vocel : **vo•cal**
vodca : **vod•ka**
vod•ka
volanteer : **vol•un•teer**
vol•a•tile
vol•ca•no
volcanoe : **vol•ca•no**
volenteer : **vol•un•teer**
volitile : **vol•a•tile**
vol•ley•ball
vollinteer : **vol•un•teer**
vollyball : **vol•ley•ball**
vol•tage
voltege : **vol•tage**
voltige : **vol•tage**
vol•ume
vol•un•teer
voluptious : **vo•lup•tu•ous**
vo•lup•tu•ous

vomet : **vom•it**
vom•it
vommit : **vom•it**
vowal : **vow•el**
vow•el
vowil : **vow•el**
vowl : **vow•el**
voy•age
voyege : **voy•age**
voyer : **voy•eur**
voy•eur

voyidge : **voy•age**
voyige : **voy•age**
voyuer : **voy•eur**
vue : **view**
vul•gar
vulger : **vul•gar**
vul•ner•a•ble
vulnerible : **vul•ner•a•ble**
vyeing : **vy•ing**
vy•ing
vynil : **vi•nyl**

Ww

waddel : **wad•dle**
  (walk like a duck);
  wat•tle (wicker)
wad•dle (walk like a
  duck); **wat•tle** (wicker)
wadle : **wad•dle**
  (walk like a duck);
  wat•tle (wicker)
wafe : **waif**
waf•er
waffel : **waf•fle**
waffer : **waf•er**
waf•fle
wafle : **waf•fle**
wagen : **wag•on**
waggon (British) : **wag•on**
wag•on
waif
waight : **weight** (mass);
  wait (expecting)
wail (cry); **whale** (animal)
wain : **wane**
wainscoat : **wain•scot**
wain•scot
waist (body); **waste** (use)

wait (expecting); **weight**
  (mass)
wait•ress
waive (forgo); **wave**
  (water; beckon)
walet : **wal•let**
wal•let
wallit : **wal•let**
wallnut : **wal•nut**
wal•nut
wal•rus
walts : **waltz**
waltz
wane
wanten : **wan•ton**
wan•ton
warant : **war•rant**
war•ble
war•den
wardon : **war•den**
ware•house
warf : **wharf**
warhouse : **ware•house**
warior : **war•ri•or**
war•rant
warrent : **war•rant**

warrier : **war•ri•or**
war•ri•or
wash•a•ble
washible : **wash•a•ble**
waste (use); **waist** (body)
wa•ter
watermelan :
  wa•ter•mel•on
watermellin :
  wa•ter•mel•on
watermellon :
  wa•ter•mel•on
wa•ter•mel•on
watress : **wait•ress**
watter : **wa•ter**
wat•tle (wicker); **wad•dle**
  (walk like a duck)
wave (water; beckon);
  waive (forgo)
weakan : **weak•en**
weak•en
wealth•y
weapen : **weap•on**
weap•on
wearas : **where•as**
wearhouse : **ware•house**
wearwolf : **were•wolf**
weasal : **wea•sel**
wea•sel
weath•er (atmospheric
  conditions);
  wheth•er (if)
weave
weazal : **wea•sel**

Wednes•day
weesel : **wea•sel**
weight (mass); **wait**
  (expecting)
weigt : **weight** (mass);
  wait (expecting)
weild : **wield**
weiner : **wie•ner**
weird
wel•come
welcum : **wel•come**
wellcome : **wel•come**
welthy : **wealth•y**
Wendesday : **Wednes•day**
Wendsday : **Wednes•day**
wepon : **weap•on**
werehouse : **ware•house**
were•wolf
werthy : **wor•thy**
wet (water); **whet**
  (sharpen)
wether : **weath•er**
  (atmospheric condi-
  tions); **wheth•er** (if)
whale (animal); **wail** (cry)
wharf
wheadle : **whee•dle**
whee•dle
wheras : **where•as**
where•as
where•ever : **wher•ev•er**
wherehouse : **ware•house**
wher•ev•er
wherewolf : **were•wolf**

whet (sharpen); **wet**
(water)

wheth•er (if); **weath•er**
(atmospheric conditions)

which (what one); **witch**
(magic woman)

whim•per

whim•si•cal

whine (wail); **wine** (drink)

whin•ny (neigh); **whiny**
(whine)

whiny (whine); **whin•ny**
(neigh)

whirl

whirl•pool

whis•key

whisky : **whis•key**

whi•sper

whissle : **whis•tle**

whis•tle

whith•er (to where);
with•er (shrivel)

whitle : **whit•tle**

whit•tle

wholely : **whol•ly**
(totally); **ho•ly** (sacred)

whole•some

whol•ly (totally); **ho•ly**
(sacred)

wholy : **whol•ly** (totally);
ho•ly (sacred)

whose (belonging to
whom); **who•s**
(contraction)

who•s (contraction);
whose (belonging
to whom)

wich : **which** (what one);
witch (magic woman)

widoe : **wid•ow**

wid•ow

wield

wie•ner

wierd : **weird**

wil•ful : will•ful

wilfull : **wil•ful : will•ful**

willful : wil•ful

willoe : **wil•low**

wil•low

wimper : **whim•per**

wimsical : **whim•si•cal**

wince

windsheild : **wind•shield**

wind•shield

wine (drink); **whine** (wail)

wirl : **whirl**

wisdem : **wis•dom**

wis•dom

wisdum : **wis•dom**

wiskey : **whis•key**

wisper : **whi•sper**

wistle : **whist•le**

witch (magic woman);
which (what one)

with•draw•al

withdrawel :
with•draw•al

withdrawl : **with•draw•al**

with•er (shrivel);
  whith•er (to where)
with•hold
withold : with•hold
wit•ness
witniss : wit•ness
wittle : whit•tle
wiz•ard
wizerd : wiz•ard
wolf
won•der•ful
wonderfull : won•der•ful
wonderous : won•drous
won•drous
wool•en; wool•len
wool•len; wool•en
wool•ly
wooly : wool•ly
worble : war•ble
wor•ship•ing :
  wor•ship•ping
wor•ship•ping :
  wor•ship•ing
wor•thy
wrath
wraught : wrought

wreak (inflict); reek
  (stink)
wreath (noun); wreathe
  (verb)
wreathe (verb); wreath
  (noun)
wreckless : reck•less
wrench
wressle : wres•tle
wres•tle
wretch (miserable person);
  retch (vomit)
wretch•ed
wrin•kle
wrist
write (mark paper); right
  (correct; not left); rite
  (custom)
writeing : writ•ing
writ•er
writ•ing
writhe
writter : writ•er
writting : writ•ing
wrought
wry (ironic); rye (grain)

Xx

xenofobia : **xe•no•pho•bia**
xenophobea :
   xe•no•pho•bia
xe•no•pho•bia
Xe•rox
xilophone : **xy•lo•phone**

X-ray
xylafone : **xy•lo•phone**
xylaphone : **xy•lo•phone**
xylephone : **xy•lo•phone**
xy•lo•phone

Yy

yacht
yack : **yak**
yaht : **yacht**
yak
yam
yamaka : **yar•mul•ke**
yamalka : **yar•mul•ke**
yamm : **yam**
yard•age
yardege : **yard•age**
yardidge : **yard•age**
yardige : **yard•age**
yarmulka : **yar•mul•ke**
yar•mul•ke
yaun : **yawn**
yawn
year
yearn
yeast
yeest : **yeast**
yeild : **yield**
yelloe : **yel•low**
yel•low
yelow : **yel•low**
yeo•man
yern : **yearn**

yestaday : **yes•ter•day**
yes•ter•day
yew (tree); ewe
   (female sheep); **you**
   (pronoun)
Yid•dish
Yidish : **Yid•dish**
yield
yodal : **yo•del**
yo•del
yodle : **yo•del**
yo•ga
yogert : **yo•gurt**
yogert : **yo•gurt**
yogha : **yo•ga**
yo•gi
yo•gurt
yoke (harness); **yolk** (egg)
yolk (egg); **yoke** (harness)
yoman : **yeo•man**
yool : **yule**
yooth : **youth**
yore (past); **your**
   (possessive); **you•re**
   (you are)
Yo•sem•i•te

Yosemity : **Yo•sem•i•te**
you (pronoun); **ewe**
  (female sheep); **yew**
  (tree)
young
your (possessive); **yore**
  (past); **you're**
  (you are)
yours
your•self
your's : **yours**

youth
you're (you are); **yore**
  (past); **your**
  (possessive)
yuc•ca
yucka : **yuc•ca**
Yuckon : **Yu•kon**
Yu•kon
yule
yurn : **yearn**

Zz

zar : **czar; tzar**
zeabra : **ze•bra**
zeal
zeal•ot

zeal•ous
ze•bra
zeebra : **ze•bra**
zeel : **zeal**
zefir : **zeph•yr**
zefyr : **zeph•yr**
zelot : **zeal•ot**
zelous : **zeal•ous**
ze•nith
zenophobia :
  xe•no•pho•bia
zepelin : **zep•pe•lin**
zepher : **zeph•yr**
zephir : **zeph•yr**
zeph•yr
zep•pe•lin
zepplin : **zep•pe•lin**
ze•ro
zerox : **Xe•rox**
zigote : **zy•gote**
zinc
zinia : **zin•nia**
zink : **zinc**
zin•nia

ziper : **zip•per**
zip•per
zir•con
zirkon : **zir•con**
zith•er
zo•di•ac
zodiack : **zo•di•ac**
zodiak : **zo•di•ac**
zology : **zo•ol•o•gy**
zom•bie
zomby : **zom•bie**
zone
zooligy : **zo•ol•o•gy**
zo•ol•o•gy
zuc•chi•ni
zuccini : **zuc•chi•ni**
zuchini : **zuc•chi•ni**
zy•gote
zylophone : **xy•lo•phone**
zyther : **zith•er**

INFORMATIVE AND
FUN READING

__THE RAINFOREST BOOK by Scott Lewis
   Preface by Robert Redford   0-425-13769-4/$3.99
Look into the spectacular world of tropical rainforests--their amazing
diversity, the threats to their survival, and the ways we can preserve them
for future generations. This easy-to-read handbook is full of practical tips
for turning your concern for rainforests into action.

__MOTHER NATURE'S GREATEST HITS
   by Bartleby Nash   0-425-13652-3/$4.50
Meet the animal kingdom's weirdest, wackiest, wildest creatures! Learn
about dancing badgers, beer-drinking raccoons, 180-foot worms, Good
Samaritan animals and more!

__FOR KIDS WHO LOVE ANIMALS by Linda Koebner
with the ASPCA   0-425-13632-9/$4.50
Where and how do animals live? How did they evolve? Why are they
endangered? Explore the wonders of the animal kingdom while you
discover how to make the Earth a safer home for all animals.

__SAFE FOOD by Michael F. Jacobson, Ph.D., Lisa Y.
Lefferts and Anne Witte Garland 0-425-13621-3/$4.99
 This clear, helpful guide explains how you can avoid hidden hazards--and
shows that eating safely doesn't have to mean hassles, high prices, and
special trips to health food stores.